Beautiful Ugly:
The Call, The Cry, The Coming

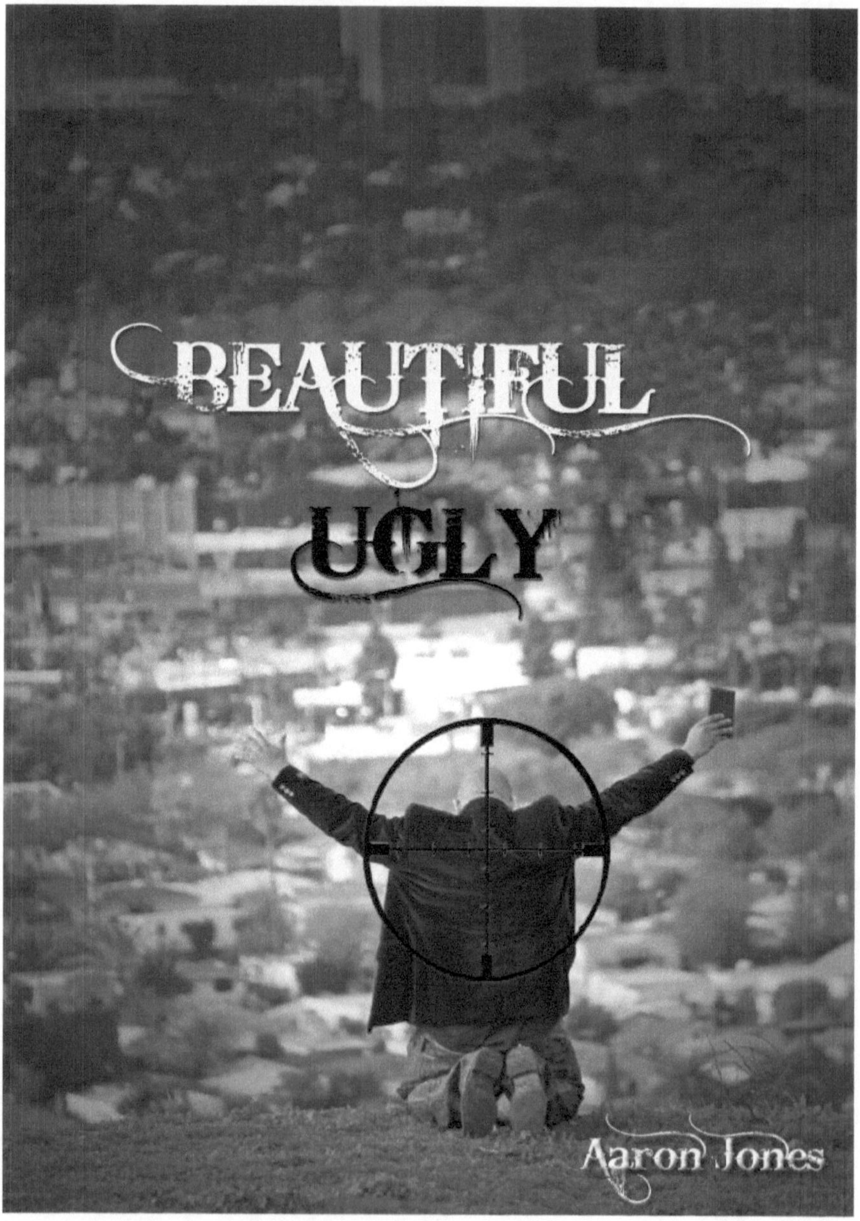
BEAUTIFUL
UGLY
Aaron Jones

Beautiful Ugly:
The Call, The Cry, The Coming

Aaron Jones

Aaron Jones Publishing
2014

First Printing: 2012

ISBN 978-1-105-25421-5

Aaron Jones Publishing

Email: itsmrjones@live.com

Dedication

Dedicated to the Father, Son, and the Holy Spirit
may I glorify you God with my life.
I can do all things through Christ which
strengtheneth me.-Philippians 4:13

Also dedicated to my good friend Gilbert Atwood
may your memory live on eternally.

Contents

Aaron Jones iii

Introduction 2

The Declaration...9

Broken Home..25

The Decision 36

A Perfect World..51

Longest War Ever 66

Immanuel...81

Who is Jesus? 93

Beautiful Ugly...105

Time to Answer 126

Power to the People...138

Neglected Love..147

Sound Doctrine...155

Lovers of Lies 165

One Name 173

The Eulogy..185

Exodus 189

Benediction...194

After these Things 211

Introduction

I beseech you therefore, brethren, by the mercies of God, that ye present your bodies a living sacrifice, holy, acceptable unto God, which is your reasonable service. And be not conformed to this world: but be ye transformed by the renewing of your mind, that ye may prove what is that good, and acceptable, and perfect, will of God.- Romans 12:1-2

It was the most beautiful of times and the ugliest of times but, through faith in Jesus Christ we survived. The world as we knew it changed and each day the wickedness increased. Yet still, we thanked God because we knew that anyone who believed in Christ Jesus would never see the worst of these days. The earth was like a woman before childbirth and her labor pains were increasing. The times in which we lived were a precursor to the birth. The child that would soon be born to mother earth would usher in the worse seven years in the earth's history.

I remember the days when many nations gathered in harmony to destroy Israel. They all had their reasons some for economic gain and others out of pure hatred. Russia, Eastern Europe, the Balkan States, Iraq, Iran, Libya, and Ethiopia gathered together to destroy our brothers and sisters in Israel. Many nations watched in observance and wondered what the outcome would be. The enemies of Israel thought a victory would be easy but their internal conflict combined with the elements striving against them made victory impossible. The armies with one mind and one purpose rose up against the children of Israel and it baffles the world to this day what happened to those armies when they tried to invade Israel.

We were not shocked all because we knew that God promised to protect Israel. The enemies of Israel fell in astronomical numbers and it took the armies of Israel seven months to bury the fallen soldiers. Many of our friends that were seeking employment were contracted by Israel to become professional gravediggers. The event was gruesome and I would receive calls from brothers and sisters in Israel that would tell me how they searched the land to cleanse it and when they would see remains of a dead body they would set up a marker next to the bodies until they were buried. The markers were used to identify the dead bodies and their locations. For seven years the weapons of the dead armies provided energy and fuel for the nation of Israel and it was that event that sparked the mind of a new enemy. This new enemy wanted to conquer the world and hated Israel with a passion.

In those days I was just a faithful minister, but soon I would become a martyr for the kingdom of Heaven. Things in America began to change once new leadership had taken over and being a Christian became frowned upon. Celebrities, news reporters, athletes, you name it everyone began to openly mock Jesus Christ. Nevertheless, I preached the gospel every chance I got and because of that my freedom has been taken. I have been imprisoned for many years but today shall be the last day of my imprisonment. Today is the day that they have scheduled me for my execution, but I pray today is the day that all believers will be raptured right before their very eyes. No matter the outcome I write this letter unto anybody that may come in my prison cell and find it. I ask that you read this collection of letters I have written to my grandchildren that you may understand who the true and living God is. I encourage you to read these letters and also to read the Holy Bible that is with these letters that you may discover the truth in these last and evil days.

In the words of the Apostle Paul "I charge thee therefore before God, and the Lord Jesus Christ, who shall judge the quick and the dead at his appearing and his kingdom; Preach the word; be instant in season, out of season; reprove, rebuke, exhort with all long suffering and doctrine. For the time will come when they will not endure sound doctrine; but after their own lusts shall they heap to themselves teachers, having itching ears; And they shall turn away their ears from the truth, and shall be turned unto fables. But watch thou in all things, endure afflictions, do the work of an evangelist, make full proof of thy ministry. For I am now ready to be offered, and the time of my departure is at hand. I have fought a good fight, I have finished my course, I have kept the faith: Henceforth there is laid up for me a crown of righteousness, which the Lord, the righteous judge, shall give me at that day: and not to me only, but unto all them also that love his appearing."

The world is experiencing some ugly times but the salvation of Jesus Christ makes any day beautiful. Read and share..........They call me Adam and this is the Beautiful Ugly

Sincerely,

Adam

The Cry

Jesus wept-John 11:35

Aaron Jones

The Declaration

O LORD, our Lord, How excellent is Your name in all the earth,

Who have set Your glory above the heavens! Out of the mouth of

babes and nursing infants You have ordained strength, Because of

Your enemies, That You may silence the enemy and the avenger.

When I consider Your heavens, the work of Your fingers, The moon

and the stars, which You have ordained, What is man that You are

mindful of him, And the son of man that You visit him? For You have

made him a little lower than the angels, And You have crowned him

with glory and honor. You have made him to have dominion over the

works of Your hands; You have put all things under his feet, All sheep

and oxen Even the beasts of the field, The birds of the air, And the fish

of the sea That pass through the paths of the seas. O LORD, our Lord,

How excellent is Your name in all the earth!-Psalm 8

To my Sons and Daughters,

I, a humble servant of Jesus Christ by the will of God write to

you children of my son, grace and peace unto you from God our

Father through our Lord and Savior Jesus Christ. They call me Adam son of Abdul, father of your father Arnold, and grandfather to many. I have longed for years to see you face to face my children and to write letters to you. I have restrained myself for your safety, but the current conditions have forced me to speak. I'm not sure what your father has told you about me but I am very much alive and I love your father with all of my heart. The last letter I received from your father he swore on the grave of my father that he would erase my name from the memory of this earth. Glory be to God for your grandmother Bethany a true woman of God who raised your father to fear the Lord in my absence and who has encouraged me to write this letter to you.

When I was a child America was known as the land of the free and the home of the brave. This country in unison said, "let freedom ring" and we stamped "In God we Trust" on our currency. We sung God bless America as we exercised our rights as Americans to worship God publically. Millions of Americans would gather from sea to shining sea and pledge allegiance to the flag and declare that we are "One nation under God." Our forefathers believed in the freedom to worship God in the way we think is the most agreeable to his will and that the freedom to choose or neglect a religion was a fundamental human right. The federal government has no authority to declare one religion right or wrong, nor to declare a state religion. This country wasn't perfect it has had its battles with immoral leaders and the greed of men, but it was as good as it gets for a country governed by imperfect men. There are many things in this country that men had to fight for but at least in those days a person was able to fight for what he or she believed in. America the beautiful land that I love; why have you allowed your children to rape and pillage you of your greatest beauty of all? - Your freedom. The freedom that we once shared as Americans has been overthrown and our ability to challenge the moral decisions of our leaders has been banned. All because the people neglected to vote their values and the church sat silent as it happened.

The church sat neutral in times of moral crisis as the New Americans demanded their civil liberties and the first item on the agenda was to ban Jesus from America and arrest all who continue to speak in his name. The church watched as all Americans 1st amendment rights were violated as it is written in The Bill of Rights *"Congress shall make no law respecting an establishment of religion, or prohibiting the free exercise thereof; or abridging the freedom of speech, or of the press; or the right of the people peaceably to assemble, and to petition the Government for a redress of grievances."*

I remember the day America changed forever, the President of the United States stood up and gave his State of the Union speech and he said "These are trying times for not only America but the world also. It is days such as these that America must not think of itself as a big player on the planet of earth but one of many players on the team of planet earth. The days of America declaring itself better than everyone else is over and the evidence of this decline is shown by the strength of our military and the power of our dollar. It is time now that America pushes toward a more global agenda and become brothers with the nations of this great planet. We are one world and one human race and for too long we have allowed differences such as race, traditions, and religious practices to divide, but no longer will this be true. In light of the recent war that has destroyed many lives in the Middle East we have to take a hard look at how the religion and faith of certain groups can be dangerous. This is no longer the times of Thomas Jefferson, Paul Bunyan, Martin Luther, Moses, or even father Abraham today is a new day with new evils that we face. We have to be careful when people call America a Christian nation because being a Christian nation is not only offensive to the beliefs of others but demeaning to the world. The lies and propaganda that Christian leaders and their Bible has spread, has affected the whole world for the negative. It is Christianity that has invented slavery, told people to murder their children if God says so, murder the husband of a woman you are in engaged in an affair with. It is Christianity that says God will send all to people to hell. The Bible is full of contradictions and hate and this is the same Bible that Adolf Hitler used in his defense. As Americans we can't sit by and watch Christianity destroy this nation as it has already destroyed others. Americans are not the weak and feeble people we once were clinging to the God of the Christians for strength. We are not one nation under God, we are one nation standing on American soil. I declare that today marks the day that one government standing on Capitol Hill shall lead America and the world to freedom, honor, and salvation. I declare that this nation shall ban all bibles and punish all who spread the lies and propaganda known as the gospel of Jesus Christ. This is our land, our country, and we shall let the world know that America is not a Christian nation but a nation of love and tolerance! The old America is dead and today I declare that this nation shall be known as New America (applause)."

Together Christians watched in silence as billboards, radio ads went up mocking Jesus Christ. The government campaigned to make the President's Proposition 666 legal in the United States. In those days my buddies and I preached our hearts out against the government but we couldn't get many churches to follow us. They were afraid to lose their tax exemption, members, and financial backing so they sat in silence. Our lives were threatened, we were beaten, but we kept preaching against the anti-Christian laws of the government. We took a stand for righteousness as we became light in a dark world but without the rest of the churches support we weren't able to put up much of a fight.

When Congress finally passed the law the President stood up that day and said "Change has come to America and no longer will Americans be forced to live under the oppression of the gospel of Jesus Christ do what you will and that shall fulfill the law of the land." The crowd erupted in cheers and all over the streets people burned down churches and shouted out "Death to the Jesus Freaks." The news called it revolution but we called it foolishness and it was clear to us that Jesus was now on the outside of the church knocking on the door but the members of the church had refused to let him in because they loved themselves more. Organized religion was still permitted just as long as Jesus was not preached or spoken of in a positive way so my father Abdul had no problem being that he practiced Islam. As for me and my younger brother Benjamin we were shocked at how many Jehovah Witnesses, Catholics, Mormons, and Evangelical Churches that had no problem complying with the law and removing Christ from their teachings.

The more this country declared the non-existence of Jesus Christ the more violent and oppressing this country became. The propaganda that the President fed the people was that removing Jesus would change this country for the better but it didn't. The economy grew worse, depression rose, and a mysterious flu began claiming the lives of many Americans. This country became a grave without color, the walking dead was its government, and instead of admitting that banning Christ was wrong this country began to blame us Christians who now worshipped underground as the source of its problems. Once again the President had to make a speech "My fellow Americans this country has suffered great difficulty and the problems began when we chose to stand up and fight against Jesus and his believers. What can I say that we were wrong? Certainly not, we were absolutely right in banning Jesus and the current chaos is our evidence. I declare that on this day anyone caught praying in the name of Jesus, teaching Christianity, or who is a believer in Christ in their heart shall be imprisoned, fined , and they won't be allowed to attend school, work, own homes, or rent property. As Chief Executive there will be no vote on this because times such as these call for Marshall Law. We will not be defeated by the witchcraft of those who follow this Jesus."

Those were the days when all the statues of our forefathers who proclaimed Jesus as their Lord were torn down and armed guards patrolled the streets looking to punish anyone who prayed in Jesus name or carried a Bible. The words of Charles Darwin, Stephen Hawkings, and Richard Dawkins were taught in school which was utter foolishness. My children the educational system has failed you by teaching you this world began by a big bang or through evolution because it is a known fact that in the beginning God created Heaven and Earth. I wish to God that the church would've taken a strong position and fought for what it believed in but the truth is the church had left its first love and began loving its own work more. The President of those days was motivated by pleasing all men and feared displeasing any in short he was ruled by his own pride. The enemies of Jesus Christ recognized his pride immediately and began to use the media to bash him in order to sway him to conform to their hidden agenda. The President began as a man of principle who believed in Jesus Christ and change for a better America and he ended up a man who changed from wanting a better America to a global government. The people praised this President not for his political stance but for his eloquence, charisma, and his ability to flatter. This President that once loved Jesus and wanted a better America had foolishly turned his back on Christ and started a Holocaust in America against all Christians.

Your father was 8 years old when the government came for me and my younger brother Benjamin. We were warned many of times not to teach in Jesus name but we refused and every week we held church in our home or in the fields. Even if we tried to shut up and stop proclaiming Christ the word of God burned like fire in our bones and we became public enemy #1 on the governments list. As Christians we would rather die than to survive like those other so called Christians who denied Christ in order to survive. I'd rather offend men and please my God than to offend my God and please mankind. Every week your grandmother would cook breakfast and believers would assemble in our home for fellowship. The night before my departure I was in deep prayer and God instructed me to broadcast tomorrow's message live on the internet for all to see and hear. The thought of this terrified me because I knew that the consequences for this action would be severe. I sat down your grandmother, uncle, and mother that night and told them what the Lord had instructed me to do and your Uncle ironically finished my sentence. The Lord had instructed him to do the same so it was agreed that we would obey. I spent that night sleeping on the floor next to your father's bed talking to him until he fell asleep telling him how much I loved him.

The next morning I stood up in the living room and stared at the eyes of every man woman and child in the room. Your uncle gave me the green light that we were live on-air and with butterflies in my stomach I began to teach. "Turn with me if you will to the book of Psalms chapter 14 beginning with verse 1. Today's message is titled "The foolish man and the house he has built." The word of the Lord reads as follows *"The fool hath said in his heart, There is no God. They are corrupt, they have done abominable works, there is none that doeth good The LORD looked down from heaven upon the children of men, to see if there were any that did understand, and seek God. They are all gone aside, they are all together become filthy: there is none that doeth good, no, not one."* Amen let us pray "Father God if you will we ask that you be glorified through this time of sharing your word. Touch the hearts of all that have risked everything to gather here and all that listen from afar, may you change the hearts of all worldwide. May you look upon this nation and call this nation to repent for their sins against you and grant them the wisdom to hearken to your cry. In Jesus name we pray and let the church say Amen.

My fellow Christians I don't have to tell you how trying these times are but I can tell you that Jesus is on our side. The war that they fight against us is a war they fight against Christ and we will not lie down and sit back while the government mocks the name of Christ. It is evident that you have chosen to risk your life for the name of Jesus and I declare to you that Jesus is the way the truth and the life...."

All of a sudden there was a loud boom and all eyes turned to the front door as officers in all black riot gear burst through firing tear gas. I rushed to protect the children as the feet of hell stomped me severely as I cried out "Jesus, Jesus," and I remember one guard saying "Jesus can't save you now." My brother Benjamin grabbed your father and tried to hide him in the bathroom. Armed guards burst through the door of the bathroom to find Benjamin and your father praying *"The LORD is my shepherd; I shall not want. He maketh me to lie down in green pastures: he leadeth me beside the still waters. He restoreth my soul: he leadeth me in the paths of righteousness for his name's sake. Yea, though I walk through the valley of the shadow of death, I will fear no evil: for thou art with me; thy rod and thy staff they comfort me. Thou preparest a table before*

me in the presence of mine enemies: thou anointest my head with oil;
my cup runneth over. Surely goodness and mercy shall follow me all
the days of my life: and I will dwell in the house of the LORD
forever." Before the Amen could come out of your father's mouth the
guards shot my brother in cold blood before the eyes of your father.
My brother was faithful to the death, he was the son of Carolyn my
mother, husband and father to none, martyr for Christ, child of God, a
man who finished his Amen in Heaven before the throne of his God.
They called him Benjamin and he was my brother.

They wrapped my face in a white cloth to shame me and hide my
identity. Your father watched with your grandmother as they carried
me away in those steel handcuffs never to see me again. We never
thought the day would come that people would be murdered in
America for proclaiming Christ but we thought wrong. Ironically, the
very same President that was manipulated into bringing this chaos
upon Americans was murdered by his own actions. He was caught
praying for his ill wife as she had become a new victim of the
mysterious flu and his Secret Service was aware of his prayers so one
day they recorded him praying. The President was arrested and before

a court of law and on live broadcast there was a video recording of the President praying in Jesus name for his sick wife to be healed.

The President was beheaded for his crimes of domestic terrorism. I sit now in prison on death row, waiting to be beheaded for domestic terrorism, treason, witchcraft, and conspiracy. Meanwhile I leave behind a son who hates God for taking away his Uncle and Father, and hates me for listening to God. I leave behind a loving wife who has lost a close connection with her son because she loves his father and the Jesus his father serves. I left behind a father who always hated me because I refused to teach your father Islam. Most importantly, I leave behind you whom I have never seen face to face, but have left to discover the truth about this world on their own. My grandchildren whose father and now deceased mother (victim of the mysterious flu) and schools have taught them to be atheist and that there is no God.

Forgive me of my absence but I am only absent because I have discovered the greatest truth known to mankind *"That if you confess with your mouth the Lord Jesus and believe in your heart that God has raised Him from the dead, you will be saved. For with the heart one believes unto righteousness, and with the mouth confession is made unto salvation. For the Scripture says, Whoever believes on Him will not be put to shame. For there is no distinction between Jew and Greek, for the same Lord over all is rich to all who call upon Him. For whoever calls on the*

name of the LORD shall be saved." They call him Jesus, fully God and fully man. Second person of the trinity, God the Son, creator of the universe, Savior of the world, and for him I risk my life and write this letter to you.

They call me Adam and I am your grandfather

Broken Home

When I was a child, I spake as a child, I understood as a child, I thought as a child: but when I became a man, I put away childish things.-1 Corinthians 13:11

To my Sons and Daughters,

"Who am I? Where have I been? What makes me the man that I am? Why do I make the decisions I make? Who is this Jesus that I serve and am willing to die for?" In due time my children I shall answer all these questions and more but for now allow me to share my soul with you. My mother (God bless her soul) almost aborted me until my grandmother (by the mercies of God) discovered that she was pregnant and convinced her to give birth. My parents were teenagers when I was conceived and my father came from a strict Sunni Islam household and my mother came from a strict Christian household. Despite their differences the two were united by lust.

When my grandfather Nazir discovered that my father was having a child he told my mother that unless she converted to Islam his son would have no dealings with her or her bastard child. My mother was too much of a free spirit to convert to Islam. She hated rules and authority and she didn't like responsibility much either. When my mother refused to convert to Islam my father abandoned her. It would be 6 years before my mother ever seen my father again. The first time I seen my father he was married with a one year old son Abdul Jr. and it was clear that I was just an afterthought. My mother kept her promise to my grandmother and as soon as I was born she gave me to her.

My grandmother named me Adam because she said I was the first. My mother moved to Berkeley, CA to attend school at UC Berkley only to return 2 years later with my brother Benjamin. I never met his father but it is believed that he became a professional football player later on in life. My grandfather was a minister of the gospel and he always took me and Benny (Benjamin) with him whenever he preached. We hated going with him but he said he was preparing us for the future. My grandfather was a great teacher of the gospel but he also taught with so much passion and conviction that you knew that the words he spoke were the words of a Living God. I always admired that about him he really loved teaching the world about Christ even if it meant his life.

My grandmother was a nurturer and the perfect balance to my strict grandfather. She never lacked compassion and had a practical way of looking at every situation. She really had a heart for dealing with those who had lost their way and I wish I had only a small piece of her compassion in my own heart. Grandma always allowed my father to come and visit and she never treated him ill or scowled at him; like my grandfather did she truly believed that one day he would change.

While my mother forsook the teachings of Christ until the day she died my father was serious about Allah and whenever I seen him he would always try and teach me about Islam. I always listened to my father for the brief moments that I spent with him but I could never grasp the concepts of Islam. After awhile my father gave up on me and decided that whatever my grandparents had taught me was instilled in me and there was no changing me. Until this day I always wondered what would have became of me and my faith had my father raised me. I always wondered what would life be like if my mother had converted to Islam and married my father.

My mother promised to come back for Benjamin and I once she finished school but tragically she died in a car accident when I was 9 years old. The crazy part about my mother's death is that since Benny and I never knew her we didn't even cry. I thank God for giving Benjamin and I such wonderful grandparents and I wish to God that I could say that I never disappointed them but eventually I did. Maybe it was all the Islam my father taught me or the rebelliousness of my mother inside of my heart but at the age of 14 I decided that God didn't exist and became an Atheist.

My freshman year in high school was very confusing; the world around me was changing quickly and the educational system had changed dramatically. The biggest change was that we no longer said the pledge of allegiance before class. We no longer prayed at the beginning of class instead we got right to our lesson. The schools were filled with violence, gangs, drugs, and dropouts but that was okay as long as we didn't bring up God in the classroom. I had a history teacher that prided himself on blaspheming God and he would teach us ancient civilizations in order to mock all religion. He told us that man made God or gods out of their own fear and imagination. At the time I was conflicted in the inside of my soul, torn between the God of my grandfather and the god of my father. Who was right? Who was going to hell and who wasn't? What faith should I choose? I was tormented daily by these thoughts until the point I began to smoke marijuana with a kid I knew from junior high named Saul.

My freshman year in high school me and Saul became best friends. We were friends in junior high but in high school we were inseparable. While smoking weed Saul would always talk about how he didn't believe in God and the stuff his father and my grandfather preached was junk man. He told me that I should spend more time talking to Dr. Smith my freshman history teacher he was a solid man who knew the truth. So everyday afterschool I would sit with Saul and Dr. Smith getting intoxicated while talking religion and god. Saul was right Dr. Smith was solid he seemed to genuinely care about us students and making sure we knew the truth and not a lie. I remember the day I began to really buy into his method of thinking he said "Adam if God existed why did he put us here? In fact Adam how do we know which God to believe in if you were born in a Buddhist home or a Hindu home wouldn't you believe in those religions? Would you then not conclude that those religions were true and all other religions false?" I was shocked he knew exactly the situation I faced at home all I can say is "I don't know sir." He replied "Think about it Adam all over the world people are born into many cultures and have many beliefs how do we decide who is right?" I admit this teacher was crafty and subtle he modeled the serpent in the garden. He wanted me to question the word of God so he can go in for the kill and he was successful momentarily.

Looking back now I probably would have told him that I would believe in God no matter what culture I was born in because it is impossible for man to exist without a creator. Even if I am wrong about my approach to God; if I diligently seek the true God I have full confidence that he would reveal himself to me. *For he that cometh to God must believe that he is, and that he is a rewarder of them that diligently seek him.* Looking back my teacher was a coward he rather play it safe and trust in his own intellect than to take the risk of seeking God and finding him. I have seen brothers from all over the world including my father's father who was a devout Muslim who converted to Christianity because he was diligently seeking God.

My grandfather Nazir attended my cousin Sayid's funeral (his grandson) who had become a believer in Christ before he died. I delivered the gospel message at Sayid's funeral and my grandfather shocked us all when he came to the faith. My grandfather coming to the faith shattered my father's faith in Islam and he spent the rest of his remaining life in confusion. People want to know the true God and because God is all powerful he won't hide himself from those who truly want to know him. There are billions of testimonies just like this from people all over the world and from every walk of life that have found Jesus to be the answer to all of their questions. My teacher had neglected a true fact that every human being was given freewill and a conscience to know right from wrong. Where a person is born has nothing to do with the decision that person makes ultimately about the God of the whole universe.

My children, one day like billions of others you will have to seek God and search for the truth. I pray that in your quest that you discover that Jesus is the way, the truth, and the life, and that no man comes to the Father except through him first. My teacher had made me question God that day because he struck home. I was in the middle of a jihad at home torn in between a Muslim family and a Christian family. I was confused as to who was right and who was wrong. My teacher passed me the joint and said "Don't let the fear of a false god prevent you from enjoying the pleasures of this world."

That night I made the decision to reject all religion and although I confessed I didn't believe in God my conscience always brought God back into my heart especially when death occurred. I tried with all my heart to enjoy my freedom as an atheist but every time I did wrong there was always guilt. I would always say I shouldn't feel guilty for these things because God doesn't exist but the guilt remained. Atheist are possibly the most miserable and stubborn people on this earth because they have gone against their own human nature in exchange for being their own God. They will ultimately discover that being God is not easy. I began to question myself asking myself what is good and what is evil, then questions about death arose and what happened after death and eventually it was too many questions left unanswered. My only hope was to drown the questions in sin which led to more guilt and more bitterness.

One Saturday night as I lay in my bed I had terrible feeling come over me a feeling that can only be described as loneliness. Truthfully,

I can't explain this feeling nor would I ever recommend feelings as a basis for faith. This is my own personal experience and that night I had a feeling come over me. I felt as if God himself had walked away from me and left me to live in this world all alone. The only problem was I didn't believe in God but that night I was definitely terrified that something worse than death was coming for me. Initially I thought maybe I had gone crazy from smoking marijuana but as my terror grew I only had one option. I grabbed my grandfathers Bible and prayed that God took this feeling away. I read the whole book of Revelation (last book in the Bible) that night with tears running down my eyes asking God to protect me, but in my heart I refused to accept that he was real. The main reason I wanted to reject God was because I didn't want to live according to his rules. I knew that being labeled a Jesus freak instantly made me an outcast and I had a rep to protect.

The next morning I went to church with my grandparents something I hadn't done in months. The whole time I was in church listening to my grandfather speaking I kept looking at Saul's mother to see if he was at church but he wasn't. I needed to talk to Saul. I needed to tell him that maybe we had been wrong and we should reconsider our position. I needed to tell Saul what happened last night but knowing Saul he would tell me I need to smoke and mellow out.

After service I changed clothes and prepared to hit the park I knew the fellas played football there every Sunday after church. I'm sure Saul was there with the fellas getting high. I rushed to the park and all I can see was a large crowd, police, and ambulance and I can hear a bunch of screaming. My buddy Lonnie spotted me and he screamed out "Adam, Adam come quick!" Lonnie was standing all the way in front of the crowd. I pushed my way through the swarms of people to see Saul lay on the ground dead. "Lonnie man what happened?" I asked. "Man, Saul was getting high with Boomer sniffing that cocaine and then he just collapsed," tears were running down Lonnie's eyes as he spoke those words. My best friend laid on the ground a lifeless corpse who died unaware of the truth and his death left me with more questions that only he could answer. I wondered why Saul decided to try the hard stuff and if I was here would I have done it too? From that day forth I never questioned if God was real it was no doubt that if I hadn't been at church that day I may have died in the park like Saul.

Throughout my life strange things like this began to happen I would get a headache and stay home only to get a phone call that someone was shot and I was supposed to be there. From that day on I never questioned if God was real I just needed to get to know God for myself.

Love,

Adam

The Decision

The word which came to Jeremiah from the LORD, saying: "Arise and go down to the potter's house, and there I will cause you to hear My words." Then I went down to the potter's house, and there he was, making something at the wheel. And the vessel that he made of clay was marred in the hand of the potter; so he made it again into another vessel, as it seemed good to the potter to make. Then the word of the LORD came to me, saying: "O house of Israel, can I not do with you as this potter?" says the LORD. "Look, as the clay is in the potter's hand, so are you in My hand, O house of Israel!-Jeremiah 18:1-6

To my Sons and Daughters,

After the death of my best friend Saul my life changed I swore off drugs forever and I developed what many call an intellectual faith in God. I knew that there was a God and in certain circumstances I depended on God to see me through such as plane rides, job interviews, or even when I'm sick but I never depended on God to run my whole life. I used God for when he was convenient for me such as to impress my grandparents, or members of the church, or even the family of girls I was interested in. In those days pulling out the Jesus card and explaining to a girl's family that I was active in a church scored me a lot of points with the parents of young ladies (may God forgive me for my foolishness). I believed in God much like I believed in your grandfather's existence. I knew God was real just like I knew my father on earth was real but I trusted neither with my whole life. Of all the people that I have known in my life it is your grandmother that has had the most impact on my life. It wasn't until God placed this miraculous woman in my life that I realized the true power of God's love and mercy and his ability to draw a man through His loving-kindness.

When I was 22 years old the world was beneath me. I felt as if I sat on the moon itself and watched the earth rotate for my own pleasure. I was fresh out of college and I had a great job as a music journalist that allowed me access to the best parties, concerts, and a whole lot of famous people. I was making a substantial amount of money for a young man my age and your grandmother was the most beautiful girlfriend a man could have. These were the days when your great grandfather exercised his greatest love toward me. Those were the days when my grandfather showed his patience toward us and allowed Benny and I to find our own path.

I was reckless; alcohol was my new best friend, partying was at the top of my agenda, and on the bottom of my agenda was church and family. Your Uncle was always a warrior for Christ since a young age and I can honestly say he never was entertained by the foolishness of the world; well at least not like I was. Every night without fail my grandfather would call me on the phone and pray with me. Despite my reckless living your great grandfather would always tell me how proud he was of me, how much he loved me, and how one day I would glorify God with my life. My grandfather loved God with all his heart and he knew the life I lived was wrong but he never gave up on me and he would always say "Adam I love you but God loves you even more than I could ever love you and his love never fails. The good book (Bible) says *"But God commended his love toward us, in that, while we were yet sinners, Christ died for us."*

Your great grandfather spoke the truth to me but there were always people around who praised me and used me for everything I had. They always preached to me the power of success, riches, and fame which always seemed to drown the words my grandfather out. My brother Benny rarely talked to me in those days unless he had to. He hated that my grandfather was loving toward me and he hated the people that I surrounded myself with. He would always tell your grandmother to leave me alone because I was bad news.

I loved your grandmother very much back then and I wanted to marry her but she refused to marry me because I didn't honor God with my life. Your grandmother loved Jesus and she loved spending time with your great grandmother which irritated me. Your great grandmother loved me but she would always tell your grandmother to find a man that honors God with his life and leave me alone. One day your grandmother did just that she left me. I guess she had enough of my foolish ways and feeling all alone I turned to the one place that had comforted me; the world. I partied hard, I partied often, I partied to I couldn't party anymore and then I partied some more.

I tried to blame my alcohol addiction, pornography addiction, and party dependency on my rough childhood and some of my childhood tragedies but at the end of the day these were just my excuses to indulge. Those things were my crutches and they never could take away any pain. In fact they only brought more pain and I quickly found my life sinking in quicksand because of my lifestyle choices. I was dying and in the midst of my agonizing death by pleasure all I could hear was your grandmother's last words echoing through the vast hallways of my soul "God has a plan for your life and that plan has a process all you have to do is be diligent and patient and God is going to work a miracle in your life when you're ready." Normally, such talk would go in one ear and out the other but for some reason her words stuck with me and I wanted nothing more than to drown her voice out. *My children there is a way which seemeth right unto a man, but the end thereof are the ways of death* and soon I would learn that God's way is in fact the only way to succeed.

It was the 4th of July my friends James, Roy, Kenny and I drove to Las Vegas from Los Angeles that morning to attend a big music event that night. The trip was a last minute decision originally I planned on spending the holiday with family and friends here in Los Angeles but my job needed me and I would do anything for my job. We planned on going to the event partying it up real good and then come home that same night. I ran into a few industry friends we ended up partying really hard with some musicians and before we knew it 4am was upon us. I told the guys that I would get them a hotel and we can sleep in Vegas and go home later on but Roy insisted that we leave for Los Angeles immediately. Roy didn't have a good time in Las Vegas he got really drunk and tried to make a pass at a young lady and to make a long story short he ended up getting into a huge fight with her boyfriend and he had enough. I was extremely tired that night and in no condition to drive but it was my car so I became the designated driver. I stopped at the gas station to get an energy drink and guzzled it down as fast as I could. I fell asleep on the road and crashed the car that night and since I was the only person wearing a seatbelt I was the only one that survived. I lost three of my closest childhood friends that night and I survived with a ruptured spleen, concussion, some bruises, a dislocated shoulder, a broken nose, and a guilty conscience.

I lay there in my hospital bed for 2 days coming in and out of consciousness and the first face that I seen in that hospital room was your grandmother's. After all I had put your grandmother through I couldn't for the love of God figure out why she would visit me but now I realize that it was the love of God that inspired her to visit me.

She asked me "Do you know for sure Adam that if you died today that you would have eternal life in heaven." I was confused and speechless I had just woken up in the hospital not sure of what really was going on and still trying to figure out why was I in the hospital. I wanted to know where my friends were and then your grandmother had the nerve to ask me a crazy question like that. "Adam if you were to die today and stand before God and he asked you why should I let you into Heaven what would your answer be?" I began to cry after she asked me those questions I really didn't have an answer I didn't know if I was going to heaven and I didn't have an answer to God as to why he should let me in. I couldn't tell God to let me in Heaven because I was a good person because I wasn't a good person in fact I never met one good person in my whole life. My grandparents were about the best people I knew but they still got angry from time to time.

Your grandmother knew that only the Holy Spirit could comfort me and out of sincere love for my soul she tried her best to help me see that what I needed the most in life was Jesus Christ. Over the next few days your grandmother would sit in the hospital with me preaching the gospel to me while I responded back to her with "Can we get back together?" Your grandmother made it perfectly clear that I had no shot at ever getting back with her but she wanted me to know Christ so she made me an offer I couldn't refuse. "Okay," she said "I'll give you one more chance but I get to pick the place that we will go to on our date." Eagerly I said "Deal," to which she replied "Okay as soon as you get out of here I expect you to be on time to take me to church on Sunday." My anger grew inside of me church was the last place I wanted to go and my grandfather's face was the last face I wanted to see. I definitely didn't want to hear any preaching from my little brother Benny about changing my ways but if I ever wanted to be with your grandmother I had to suck it up for the greater good.

A month later I got out the hospital and made good on my promise to your grandmother and we went to church together. People began to hug me and tell me how much they missed me but in my mind they were judging me and secretly saying how big of a loser I was. I felt judged and condemned but it was my own guilt that was weighing heavy on my heart because the people at the church had showed me nothing but love. My grandfather opened his Bible and he began to preach "Turn with me to Luke chapter 15 verses 11 through

32 and it reads Then He said: "A certain man had two sons. And the younger of them said to *his* father, 'Father, give me the portion of goods that falls *to me.*' So he divided to them *his* livelihood. And not many days after, the younger son gathered all together, journeyed to a far country, and there wasted his possessions with prodigal living. But when he had spent all, there arose a severe famine in that land, and he began to be in want. Then he went and joined himself to a citizen of that country, and he sent him into his fields to feed swine. And he would gladly have filled his stomach with the pods that the swine ate, and no one gave him *anything.* "But when he came to himself, he said, 'How many of my father's hired servants have bread enough and to spare, and I perish with hunger! I will arise and go to my father, and will say to him, "Father, I have sinned against heaven and before you, and I am no longer worthy to be called your son. Make me like one of your hired servants."" "And he arose and came to his father. But when he was still a great way off, his father saw him and had compassion, and ran and fell on his neck and kissed him. And the son said to him, 'Father, I have sinned against heaven and in your sight, and am no longer worthy to be called your son.' "But the father said to his servants, 'Bring out the best robe and put *it* on him, and put a

ring on his hand and sandals on *his* feet. And bring the fatted calf here and kill *it,* and let us eat and be merry; for this my son was dead and is alive again; he was lost and is found.' And they began to be merry. "Now his older son was in the field. And as he came and drew near to the house, he heard music and dancing. So he called one of the servants and asked what these things meant. And he said to him, 'Your brother has come, and because he has received him safe and sound, your father has killed the fatted calf.' "But he was angry and would not go in. Therefore his father came out and pleaded with him. So he answered and said to *his* father, 'Lo, these many years I have been serving you; I never transgressed your commandment at any time; and yet you never gave me a young goat that I might make merry with my friends. But as soon as this son of yours came, who has devoured your livelihood with harlots, you killed the fatted calf for him.' "And he said to him, 'Son, you are always with me, and all that I have is yours. It was right that we should make merry and be glad, for your brother was dead and is alive again, and was lost and is found. Let us pray." My anger grew instantly after my grandfather read those scriptures because I believed he purposely was trying to humiliate me before the congregation but it wasn't the case. My grandfather taught the Bible line upon line precept upon precept and the church had been going through the book of Luke verse by verse and it just so happened on that day I was there.

My grandfather continued to speak and the more he preached the more I realized that it wasn't him I had the problem with. My problem was with the Word of God because the Holy Spirit was convicting my soul. I have a grandfather who loves me and has made provisions for me that whatever I asked from him he gave me. In fact it was my grandfather who paid the money for my college, and paid 6 months of my rent in New York City while I interned to get this wonderful job that I have now. My grandfather loved me enough that he wanted me to pursue my dreams. He wished I would have been more like Benny and joined the ministry but he knew that wasn't going to happen.

Here I am now much like this lost son wallowing in the pig pen broken from the death of my friends and it was clear that it was time for me to come home. My grandfather loved me but as he always told me God loved me even more. Even though I turned my back on God he was waiting for me to come home much like the father of this lost son. At that moment I felt as if everyone in the room disappeared and the words of my grandfather's sermon grew louder. I could hear the passion spew from his loud raspy voice as he spoke "No person in this world is perfect but Jesus wants to perfect you. In fact Jesus said for us to be perfect even as our Father in Heaven is perfect. This means that Jesus Christ will stop at nothing to perfect our lives and it is his job to make us perfect. It is our job to surrender our life to Jesus and allow him to work on us. Eventually when it is all said and done we will look like Jesus and be able to stand before the Father in Heaven as people that have been conformed to the image of Christ. I know you have tried to be good in the past only to come up short but you lack the capability as a human being to be perfect. Therefore you must change and evolve become something more than a man you must become spiritual and learn to walk in the Spirit. The only way for this to happen is for us to die to ourselves and allow Jesus to begin a new work. In other words you and I must be born again.

Today we have to begin a new life in Christ and it won't be easy but I can guarantee that if we commit to Christ today; eternal life will be ours. We can know for sure that we have eternal life today because the word of God promised it. We will never have any doubt about our eternal security while living on this earth if you give your heart to Jesus today. This may be our last time to accept Christ because tomorrow is not promised."

My grandfather stood there with sweat dripping down his forehead wiping himself with his favorite towel, the organ began to play and the choir began to sing "This may be your last time, This may be your last time, This may be your last time, It may be your last time I don't know." I had a lump in my throat and I became very anxious inside and I wasn't sure why. My grandfather said "The doors of the church are now open anyone that wished to receive Christ today let them do so now." He extended his arm as the ministers came forward to offer prayer for all who came up to receive Christ and without thinking I made the decision that today was the day. I walked down that aisle with a purpose that day. I had heard the gospel a million times but I thank God that he gave me a million and one chances to receive him. I began the journey of a lifetime that day I was marred broken piece of clay. That day God began to build a new work of art and he built me with purpose. Thank God for your grandmother because in those early years of my journey she walked with me every step of the way and helped me become the proper leader of our home that God had created me to be.

That day I wasn't the only one who cried my younger brother Benny cried tears. I presumed they were tears of joy but years later he told me what happened. Benny had realized that he was much like the other brother in the story of the lost son he was angry because of how I had been treated and his anger had blinded him from the love of God. That day Benny learned that all along he had the blessings of God on his side and he had been selfish in trying to keep me away from that blessing because he deemed me unworthy. My brother had rather see me burn in hell than to receive the inheritance of the fathe,r because of the foolish decisions I had made but that day he learned mercy and he learned forgiveness. I died that day at the cross of Jesus Christ and I was born again a new man one that was not ruled by his human nature but was now submissive to the Spirit of God. This truly was life after death.

Sincerely,

Adam

A Perfect World

In the beginning was the Word, and the Word was with God, and the Word was God.-John 1:1

To my Sons and Daughters,

The walls of this prison surround me and they remind me every day that I have exchanged my worldly freedom for freedom in Jesus Christ. I am the caged bird that sings. I sit physically restrained in a cell but the praises that flow from my heart set me free. I am the caged bird that sings, that is physically restrained to a cell but the Lord has set my spirit free. I am the caged bird that sings and Jesus Christ has given me life and life more abundantly. I'm caged in a cell for 23 hours a day as if I'm a wild animal but my mind ventures back to the beginning of the world where men needed no shelter from the elements. The sky was man's ceiling and man lived a life were walls didn't exist. I lay on a cement floor that has caused my back to hunch but my mind ponders on the days when men lay in the field and where comforted by the creation of the Lord. Through my window each morning I gaze at the east as the sunrises and shines light upon my skin only to dream of the days when sunsets were perfect and unharmed by the pollutions of human nature. The first man on this earth would be brought to tears if he could see the way this world is today. The world we live in was once perfect but I'm afraid that the actions of mankind have changed this world for the worst. The pride of mankind has led him to declare himself the highest of all living but it is God that has measured the waters in the hollow of His hand and measured heaven with a span. God calculated the dust of the earth in a measure and weighed the mountains in scales and the hills in a balance. The nations *are* as a drop in a bucket, and are counted as the small dust on the scales in the eyes of God. *It is* He who sits above the circle of the earth, and its inhabitants *are* like grasshoppers. God stretches out the heavens like a curtain, and spreads them out like a tent to dwell in. How foolish of humans to think that we are more superior than God as if we had the capacity to teach God anything or show him something new. We are foolish enough to think that our science and research is actually progressive when in reality if we just sought God for the answers we would have a better world. I serve the God of all living and there is nothing too hard for him. My God created the whole earth perfect and without flaw in a literal six days and on the seventh day he rested from his work and seen that it was good. I tell you the truth if it pleased God he could've created this world in less than 1/1000th of a second but he was patient and showed mankind the value of working toward your goal. The world today is a shell of its former self a decline of what it once was and if we only looked at the history of the earth we would understand that technology may have increased but this world has not evolved but actually regressed. God created the earth with a perfect climate and an even temperature covered the earth, and mankind needed no protection from the elements save his own skin. He had no need of clothes for his very body clothed his true nature which was his spirit and as long as his spirit was covered man knew no shame. This was a glorious world where death did not exist and lions and tigers were but helpers to human beings. There was no need for rain because the dew provided the moisture for every plant. The beautiful oceans and landscapes free of toxins and pollutions were in abundance and man enjoyed them all.

The variety of plants and animals were only a reflection of my God's imagination and we can only imagine the things we have lost in this regression caused by sin. How times have changed since the first Adam and how cowardly do men live in the former paradise that God made specifically for him. God custom designed the world for mankind and God placed man in this world after he finished creating it. God created this world for men to enjoy but now he hears the cries of men when they say, "If there is a God why is there so much suffering in the world? If there is a God why do people die? If there is a God why are there natural disasters?" Yet still when I hear men raise such questions in an attempt to argue that God must not exist I then ask them "If God doesn't exist then are we to blame for these tragedies? If God doesn't exist then why do we expect the world to be perfect? From what perspective do you draw such questions that the world isn't functioning correctly?"

For those questions men have no answer other than God must exist. God created a perfect world but something must have happened because even in the heart of the unbeliever there is still a sense that something in this world is not quite right. Before the world ever began there was God and when I say God I mean Father, Son, and Holy

Spirit these three are one God yet they are three distinct persons. The best way that I can explain it is that we are one family yet we are many and God is Father, Son, and Holy Spirit yet together they are one God. For God is their title and they share that title equally as one and are in constant agreement with each other.

I'm sorry to have confused you but even with an explanation this is still something that you will have to believe by faith and recognize that God is so awesome that all things about him can't be understood by our small brains. I love you children and not only because you are of my own flesh and blood but because I choose to love you and that is what makes love true. In order for love to be real there must always be a choice present. I can choose to love you or choose to neglect you. I love your grandmother with all of my heart and out of all the women in the world (and believe me there are plenty of them) I chose your grandmother and that makes our bond special.

Your father my precious son my love for him will never change even though he has made it clear that he has no love for me and I respect his choice because it is his right to choose. When God created the first Adam he gave him the ability to choose between serving God or serving himself. Since Adam wasn't forced to love God then whatever choice he made would be a genuine choice. God created man to love him but God wanted mankind's love for him to be authentic. In order for our love to be authentic God gave us the freedom to choose but sadly we abused this freedom.

This country was founded on those same principles that freedom would ring and every man would have freedom to choose in America but we soon found that the heart is deceitful above all things, and desperately wicked. God would never control the heart of man only encourage men to make the better decision. God can't be blamed for the evil that sin brings upon the world and God can't be blamed for sending men to heaven or hell because it is our responsibility to choose where we want to spend eternity. The culprit behind all of this hate and malice is not a man, race, or social class. It is and always has been the serpent, the deceiver who deceived our first mother in paradise and has been destroying the creation of God ever since. He seen that God had given men freewill and took advantage of it and we must always remember that we wrestle not against flesh and blood, but against principalities, against powers, against the rulers of the darkness of this world, against spiritual wickedness in high places.

The world we live in is filled with its cruel slavery, its drug cartels, and gang violence. Every race is guilty of destroying this earth. When men drop chemicals and atomic bombs on other men we have a serious problem. We have learned to kill our brothers in more and more sophisticated ways ever since the first murder committed by our distant brother Cain who killed our distant brother Abel.

This world and this America with all the murders that it has committed have left the blood of its dead crying from beneath the dirt. There is nobody to blame but ourselves for we are all guilty of sin. Therefore the only way to fix this New America is to denounce sin and give our will over to God and allow him to lead us. When I think about prostitution, child molestation, rape, polygamy, fornication, and bestiality how could I not cry that we need to forsake our will and follow the will of God. God gave us freedom but we have abused that freedom which will be our demise eventually.

Just to think it all began in the Garden of Eden with one simple rule and one simple act of disobedience. Eve was in the garden alone when the serpent or the devil subtly appeared before her and asked her the first question in recorded time "Has God said that you shall not eat of every tree of the garden." The question of the serpent was broad and it had a little truth and a lot of lie behind it. God had commanded Adam not to eat of the fruit from the tree of the knowledge of good and evil and in turn Adam spread the word of God like an evangelist to his wife. The truth is God only said one tree was forbidden to be eaten but the rest of the trees in the garden were okay to eat.

Now our mother (bless her heart) engaged in a conversation with the serpent which I strongly advise that none of you do and she proceeded to tell the serpent "We may eat of the fruit of the trees in the garden but the tree in the middle of the garden (the tree of knowledge of good and evil) we shall not eat from it or touch it unless we die." Adam instructed Eve well in the word of God and she knew that she shouldn't eat from the tree but she made a mistake that so many others make and they pay for it dearly. She added to the word of God and the serpent took advantage. God instructed them not to eat of the tree but Eve added in that they shouldn't touch it either which was not true. It would take volumes of letters for me to explain to you the treachery and pain that has taken place from people adding and taking away from the word of God. I have seen many souls destroyed from this and many lives taken all at the hands of people who have mishandled the word of God. Now satan disguised as a serpent begins to form his attack upon Eve and pay attention because not much has changed.

The serpent told Eve "you shall not die if you eat this fruit," this was his way of challenging the authority of God which he will do in your life. The serpent then proceeded to say "God knows that the day you eat the fruit from the tree that your eyes shall be opened and you shall be as gods knowing good and evil." This attack was threefold he questioned the authority of God, he denied the danger of disobeying God, and he promised Eve an advantage or some gain from her disobedient behavior. There is no advantage in disobeying God and there is a serious consequence in being disobedient.

Temptation has a way of alluring you and obscuring your view of right from wrong. The danger of temptation is that you begin to justify your carnal desires in your mind until they seem like the right thing to do. The serpent was winning at this point because Eve never had experience with a tempter and this was a temptation that was like none other. She already committed the first mistake by giving a listening ear to the serpent and put herself at great disadvantage. God had given Eve the whole world and all he asked in return is that one tree be off limits for consumption. The serpent had convinced Eve that God was holding back from her and she should see what she has been missing.

My dear children God has withheld nothing good from us and his commandments are only to protect us and give us life more abundantly but many chase the dreams and illusions of the serpent and their end is nothing short of a tragedy. The serpent had Eve where he wanted her, she was questioning the validity of God's word, questioning his authority, doubting her own beliefs, believing that God was holding back from her, and fallen victim to three weak spots. Our brother John said it best "For all that is in the world, the lust of the flesh, and the lust of the eyes, and the pride of life, is not of the Father, but is of the world" The three weak spots are the most common form of satan's attack against us: the lust of the flesh, the lust of the eyes, and the pride of life and Eve had found herself powerless against them. Eve saw that the tree of knowledge of good and evil was good for food (the lust of the flesh), and she saw that the tree was pleasant to the eyes (lust of the eyes), and she believed that the power of the tree would make her wise like God (the pride of life) and she ate the fruit just as so many of us do today. The three weaknesses my children defeat us more times than they should and the only power against this is the word of God. Soon after Eve had decided to disobey God she spread the serpent's message with Adam. Adam in willful disobedience decided that it was in his best interest to disobey the command of God as well and he also ate the forbidden fruit. Only God knows why Adam would make such a decision but sin always gives us a good reason to justify our actions. Adam was fully aware that eating the fruit of this tree meant death as deceitful as sin is he could've said "I love my wife and I shall die with her."

Understand one thing sin will always give us an excuse to indulge in it but under no circumstances is sin the right action to take. If it is one thing I know about disobedience it is that it is very contagious. Quite often those around us that live in disobedience are much more comfortable being in disobedience with others rather than being alone and the behavior begins to spread. When a person knows to do good but decides not to do good that person has committed a sin and God promised that sin would bring death. This sinful act between our first parents created the greatest perversion to mankind in the history of our existence and as God promised life as they knew it would die and cease to exist. Our parents experienced things that had never been experienced before such as the consciousness of being naked or uncovered. Just like the animals the skin that we were in was good enough to cover the soul but now our parents believed our physical bodies demanded some type of covering.

Before sin the spirit ruled the body and the physical body was nothing more but a covering for the soul and the spirit. However after the fall the spiritual nature of man died and the physical nature of man became more dominant and more important and from here on out the body would be in control. The spiritual man inside of us connected with God because God is Spirit and those that worship him must worship him in spirit and in truth. The human body or the outer shell was just for our existence in this physical world and it was of little significance but once we sinned the body began to die slowly but surely.

Adam and Eve sewed fig leaves together in attempt to cover their newly discovered naked bodies as the glory of the Lord had departed from them and when they heard God coming in the garden of Eden they hid themselves from God. Sin will kill your prayer life and your ability to effectively communicate with God. Sin will seriously harm your relationship with God until that sin has been justified or made right before the eyes of God through the sacrifice of the cross. Never before had Adam and Eve been ashamed to see God or speak with God until that day but God in all of his love came to see his creation not in anger but in love and he wanted to know the truth. God was seeking a confession from them but in return he got excuses and finger pointing. Adam blamed Eve for his sin, Eve blamed the serpent, and the serpent well the serpent didn't get a chance to explain his side he was guilty but so were our parents.

Adam and Eve both knew the commandments of God and they both decided to break the commandments of God and as a result death must enter the world. People often ask if God exist why is there so much trouble in the world, and the answer is sin. It's nobody's fault but human beings we corrupted this earth through our own actions. When the innocent die, when sickness kills, when natural disasters destroy it's all the result of the world being separated from God because of sin. When God promised that death would come he never said how it would come. When we see the tragedies and the heartbreak of today we could only but wish that people took the word of God more seriously. I know it is hard for us to accept such painful thinking but God created a perfect world and gave it to us and it was up to us to be responsible enough to take care of it and we didn't. Adam and Eve from whom all living human beings came from gave us an inheritance that we wish we didn't have to inherit and it is called sin. The truth is none of us are innocent we are all sinners therefore death continues to breed and the perfect world God gave us has been brought to ruin. God in his love toward us had a plan to restore man back to his spiritual form and give mankind the perfect world he was originally created to live in.

When Eve blamed the serpent for her sin before the serpent could speak God began to bring judgment on him. God cursed the serpent forever and then God promised the serpent that between him and the seed of the woman that there would be war. God promised that the seed of the woman would bruise the head of the serpent and the serpent would bruise his heel. God referred to the seed of the woman which was a reference to a child that would be born miraculously since women didn't naturally carry seeds. This child that would be born would be God himself, the son of God. Jesus Christ is his name and he would become a man to save us from this fallen world. I will say of Jesus that he did in fact bruise the head of the serpent on one great day and in the process his heel or his human form (because it was lower than his Godly form) was also bruised and he did it not out of obligation but because he loves us. When people say God must not love us because he left us in this sinful world; I say on the contrary God truly loves us because he punished himself in order to save us from this sinful world. In fact all the bitterness, pain, and tragedies from this earth will be erased from our memories in the paradise of God and we will know nothing of this tragic life only a life of bliss and joy. We began a deeper and more difficult relationship with God that day. We began a relationship that causes us to experience hard and difficult times but to still trust in God no matter what. That day man would truly begin to discover his commitment or lack of commitment to God and also truly how far the love of God would go to save man from his own deceit. God removed man from the Garden of Eden but one day my children and hopefully that day is soon that which was taken from us shall be given back.

Sincerely,

Adam

Longest War Ever

You therefore must endure hardship as a good soldier of Jesus Christ. No one engaged in warfare entangles himself with the affairs of this life, that he may please him who enlisted him as a soldier.-2 Timothy 3:4-5

To my Sons and Daughters,

Comfort, comfort, comfort thank God that in these chains comfort has not forsaken our soul. As servants of the most high God we are instructed to *"be submissive to our masters with all fear, not only to the good and gentle, but also to the harsh. For this is commendable, if because of conscience toward God one endures grief, suffering wrongfully. For what credit is it if, when we are beaten for our faults, we take it patiently? But when we do good and suffer, if we take it patiently, this is commendable before God. For to this we were called, because Christ also suffered for us, leaving us an example, that we should follow His steps: "Who committed no sin, Nor was deceit found in His mouth"; who, when He was reviled, did not revile in return; when He suffered, He did not threaten, but committed Himself to Him who judges righteously; who Himself bore our sins in His own body on the tree, that we, having died to sins, might live for righteousness by whose stripes we were healed. For we were like sheep going astray, but have now returned to the Shepherd and Overseer of our souls."*

Today we find ourselves living in chains or under the constant threat of persecution and death. Why do they threaten our lives because we told them Jesus loves them? Why do they steal our freedom because we told them that God forgives all sin? Or maybe they simply hate us because we told them the truth that all man are sinners and need to repent? If it is one thing I've learned about mankind is that mankind hates to be wrong and more than anything people hate being told that they are sinners but it is the truth. *For all have sinned, and come short of the glory of God.* In times such as these it is necessary to stay focused but many of my peers have often talked of revolution. Day in and day out I hear talk of arming ourselves with weapons and waging war against our enemies. Although it is natural for man to defend himself, and at any given moment I am ready to protect the lives of others around me if need be but to take arms and wage war against our enemies is asinine. Who do we wage war against the armies of Babylon that grow stronger by the day? Seems like a logical choice since they have vowed to destroy all Christians and all countries that stand in their way of conquering the whole world. Do we wage war against B.A.D. (Babylonian Armed Defense)? Seems possible since in the name of their leader (whom they call the great Red Dragon) has waged a personal war against all religions. These insurgents hide in plain sight in countries all over the world strapping themselves with bombs and blowing up anything that stands in their way. Do we wage war against New America and its government that has decided that Christianity is domestic terrorism and the preaching of the gospel of Jesus Christ is pure evil? Do we wage war against our fellow humans who stand by silently and allow this injustice to take place?

I tell you children as I have told my comrades if we take up arms there's not a gun built in this world that can destroy the evil that lies in the hearts of men. It's going to take more than machine guns to stop our enemy it's going to take a lot of prayer and the actions of our Lord Jesus to end this war. These days are of great difficulty but the sacrifice of our savior Jesus Christ upon that cross has guaranteed that the end of our days will be more glorious than the beginning. The difficulty that we face now is looking into the eyes of our oppressors and seeing them for who they are. They are all lost souls who need the gospel of Jesus Christ more than we do. Our oppressors are not our enemies they are puppets that have been used as pawns by our great enemy. Our enemy has turned people against us so that we won't use our gospel to turn people against him. People aren't the enemy *for we do not wrestle against flesh and blood, but against principalities, against powers, against the rulers of the darkness of this age, against spiritual hosts of wickedness in the heavenly places.* Our enemy is spiritual and his very fallen nature resides in the heart of men who follow his path.

You can't shoot a spirit and certainly can't shoot the desires of men with earthly guns; for the weapons of our warfare are not carnal but mighty in God for pulling down strongholds. New America has given birth to a lewd and godless culture and with the current threats of B.A.D. and the Babylonian Empire upon us I feel that America will meet its demise. I pray and hope for your sake and mines that this is a wakeup call and New America turns to Jesus in this time of crisis.

Never before my children have I dreamed of seeing such days on earth but one thing I know for sure is that Jesus is still on the throne. Jesus will save us and if he doesn't come immediately, I am confident he will come soon to rescue those who call upon his name.

We are at war my children; it is the world vs. Jesus Christ and we all must choose a side. My prayer is that you choose to fight alongside Jesus in this war against evil. This war is the longest war to ever be fought and it began before the first human (Adam) was created and placed on earth. This war began when an angel named Lucifer decided to rebel against our God who created him and as a result he was cast down from Heaven along with 1/3 of all the angels and it has been war between satan and the creation of God ever since.

The prophet Isaiah spoke of his demise when he wrote *"How art thou fallen from heaven, O Lucifer, son of the morning! how art thou cut down to the ground, which didst weaken the nations! For thou hast said in thine heart, I will ascend into heaven, I will exalt my throne above the stars of God: I will sit also upon the mount of the congregation, in the sides of the north: I will ascend above the heights of the clouds; I will be like the most High. Yet thou shalt be brought down to hell, to the sides of the pit."*

The prophet of the Lord Ezekiel spoke of his rebellion when he wrote *"Thus saith the Lord GOD; Thou sealest up the sum, full of wisdom, and perfect in beauty. Thou hast been in Eden the garden of God; every precious stone was thy covering, the sardius, topaz, and the diamond, the beryl, the onyx, and the jasper, the sapphire, the emerald, and the carbuncle, and gold: the workmanship of thy tabrets and of thy pipes was prepared in thee in the day that thou wast created. Thou art the anointed cherub that covereth; and I have set thee so: thou wast upon the holy mountain of God; thou hast walked up and down in the midst of the stones of fire. Thou wast perfect in thy ways from the day that thou wast created, till iniquity was found in thee. By the multitude of thy merchandise they have filled the midst of thee with violence, and thou hast sinned: therefore I will cast thee as profane out of the mountain of God: and I will destroy thee, O covering cherub, from the midst of the stones of fire. Thine heart was lifted up because of thy beauty, thou hast corrupted thy wisdom by reason of thy brightness: I will cast thee to the ground, I will lay thee before kings, that they may behold thee. Thou hast defiled thy* sanctuaries by the multitude of thine iniquities, by the iniquity of thy traffick; therefore will I bring forth a fire from the midst of thee, it shall devour thee, and I will bring thee to ashes upon the earth in the sight of all them that behold thee. All they that know thee among the people shall be astonished at thee: thou shalt be a terror, and never shalt thou be any more."

The Apostle John spoke of his demise when he wrote this *"And there appeared a great wonder in heaven; a woman clothed with the sun, and the moon under her feet, and upon her head a crown of twelve stars: And she being with child cried, travailing in birth, and pained to be delivered. And there appeared another wonder in heaven; and behold a great red dragon, having seven heads and ten horns, and seven crowns upon his heads. And his tail drew the third part of the stars of heaven, and did cast them to the earth: and the dragon stood before the woman which was ready to be delivered, for to devour her child as soon as it was born. And she brought forth a man child, who was to rule all nations with a rod of iron: and her child was caught up unto God, and to his throne. And the woman fled into the wilderness, where she hath a place prepared of God, that they should feed her there a thousand two hundred and threescore days. And there was war in heaven: Michael and his angels fought against the dragon; and the dragon fought and his angels, And prevailed not; neither was their place found any more in heaven. And the great dragon was cast out, that old serpent, called the Devil, and Satan, which deceiveth the whole world: he was cast out into the earth, and his angels were cast out with him."*

Jesus Christ himself said *"I saw Satan fall like lightning from heaven."* The devil has fallen from his natural state and he will never be restored again and since his fall he has been on a mission to steal, kill, and destroy the children of God. The devil is a liar, murderer, thief, accuser, and a deceiver. One of his greatest weapons is doubt and he has great ability in using that weapon to destroy the lives of mankind. There is a war going on my children that no man is safe from but all must participate in it. The battleground is your body and the war has been waged for your soul. God gave me this new life *I was dead in my trespasses and sins as you and many others are. I walked according to the course of this world and according to the prince of the power of the air who now works in the children of disobedience. By nature since the fall in the garden we have been enslaved by our desire to fulfill the lust of the flesh, the lust of the eyes, and the pride of life and naturally we were born children of wrath. God who is rich in mercy because of His great love with which he loved us even when we were dead in trespasses, made us alive together in the heavenly places in Christ Jesus, that in the ages to come He might show the exceeding riches of His grace in His kindess toward us in Christ Jesus. For by grace I have been saved through faith, and that not of myself; it is the gift of God, not of works unless anyone should boast. For we are his workmanship, created in Christ Jesus for good works, which God prepared beforehand that we should walk in them.*

The devil is the god of this age and *he has blinded the minds of the people, who do not believe, lest the light of the gospel of the glory of Christ, who is the image of God, should shine on them. The world system is corrupt because he is corrupting it, and people are corrupt because they have doubted Christ and left themselves at will to the control of the enemy. At any given moment we can be attacked in this war even when we are in a room all alone but we must be sober and be vigilant because our adversary the devil, as a roaring lion, walketh about, seeking whom he may devour.* The truth is this war is spiritual and if you decide to join our side in this fight you must, *be strong in the Lord, and in the power of his might. Put on the whole armour of God, that ye may be able to stand against the wiles of the devil. For we wrestle not against flesh and blood, but against principalities, against powers, against the rulers of the darkness of this world, against spiritual wickedness in high places.*

We are human beings made and designed to inhabit this physical world and we are no match for angels. The only way to defeat our enemy is to call on our God and depend on him for the victory. The enemy is not stupid, he knows the power of our faith and because of that the enemy seeks to destroy our trust in God with doubt. Jesus has power over all creation including the devil and all the angels and because of that the demons tremble because they know the truth.

The devil believes in God because he has lived with God but he wants to have humans believe that God doesn't exist. The devil fears God and the protection that God gives his own children. The devil hates Jesus Christ because Jesus has defeated satan through his sacrifice on the cross so the devil tries to convince the world that Jesus doesn't exist, or he was just a man, or he was an angel, but the truth is Jesus is the all powerful Son of God. Any power that man may have in this war is always found in our submission to Jesus Christ and we must reject our desires to disobey God.

We have been commanded by Jesus who is our general to stand and not lose our ground and to be soldiers fully equipped for the fight and ready to fight. We are more than just people that have refused to be conquered by evil. We are conquerors better yet we are more than conquerors through Him who loved us. I live in this prison in chains physically and I have been starved almost to death, beat until I lost hearing in my right ear and my left eye has a permanent blood clot in it. They attack me for my testimony but I attack them with my testimony. Many souls have been set free in this prison and I have made this prison my own personal battleground. In reality I am free and those that bind me in chains are the ones who are bound by chains. My goal is to witness to them until the day they are set free and join the fight with me. My life is under constant threat and death is coming for me but I will not compromise my faith in order to gain temporary life on earth. I'd be a liar if I say that the enemy has not placed thoughts in my mind of giving up and recanting my testimony.

I remember my buddy James who was faithful unto the Lord but as those guards began to torture him by way of water boarding. He gave up the fight and declared that Jesus didn't exist only to die not even two minutes later. That image has stuck with me and others because our brother was two minutes away from the greatest place ever. He was two minutes away from heaven and he gave up and I pray that I keep the faith until the end. Whether he went to Heaven or not that is God's business but I want my oppressors to see my face on the day of my death and see the eyes of a man who died for his Jesus. My hope is that God be glorified by my death and men will be persuaded to join the army of Christ because of it. I've seen others in their fight remain neutral and say nothing but no matter what the circumstance we preach the gospel.

My children I get excited about this war for everyday a battle awaits and sometimes it is a battle between me and my old desires and those are extremely hard. I stand therefore, having my loins girt about with truth, and having on the breastplate of righteousness for my savior is true and his righteousness covers me. He is against the unrighteousness of sin and against all lies and liars and when he covers me I must take on his values as my own. My feet are shod with the preparation of the gospel of peace for my Jesus is peace and he is the only peace in this fallen world. Jesus is against all strife and chaos and when he covers me I take on his character of peace and I bring peace wherever I go. Above all I take the shield of faith, wherewith I am able to quench all the fiery darts of the wicked because Jesus is the true and faithful witness and he cast out all doubt and when he covers me I take on his character therefore I have complete faith in him to destroy any attack against my soul. I take the helmet of salvation for Christ is my salvation who protects from the judgment that his enemies shall face and I keep my mind guarded at all times with the truth that he covers me and I belong to him and how powerful His sacrifice was for me. I take the sword of the Spirit, which is the word of God; for my Jesus is the word of God and it is the word of God where all my power and strength lies. It is the word of God that judges satan and the word of God that has all authority over men and spirits.

When Jesus covers me he puts his word in me and the Holy Spirit calls his word to remembrance so that I am ready to attack all slander and deception that falls from the mouth of the enemy. My children, my spiritual armor is Jesus Christ and it is him that I want people, angels, and all spirits to see when they see me. I pray always my children because prayer gives me direction, replenishes my soul, and changes my life from day to day. Prayer is my connection with my God and it is in prayer that I am able to rise up and be bold for the kingdom of God. When I go to prayer I pray Our Father which art in Heaven to acknowledge my Father and his position on the throne. I reverence his very name and acknowledge that it is a sacred name and a name above all names hallowed be thy name. I acknowledge his Kingdom and understand that it is coming and I ask for it to come soon and for his will to be done on earth above all wills thy Kingdom come thy will be done on earth as it is in heaven. Then I pray not only for myself but for all residents of the Kingdom that God provide for us our daily bread that we will have the resources we need to be about our Fathers business each day. Then I forgive those who operate for the enemy so that they too may have a chance to be saved and also I forgive my brothers and sisters who have done me wrong and ask that God forgive me for the wrong I have done.

I ask the Lord to protect me and all of my brothers and sisters for the evil that awaits us and the temptations that are coming after us that he sustains us in our trials because all power is His and all authority and he shall reign forever and I agree with Him Amen. I love you my children and my prayer is that you join our side of the fight in time until then kiss your grandmother for me I love you.

Sincerely,

Adam

Immanuel

The thief does not come except to steal, and to kill, and to destroy. I have come that they may have life, and that they may have it more abundantly.-John 10:10

To my Sons and Daughters,

Merry Christmas, Merry Christmas, Merry Christmas, oh my children this is my favorite time of the year. Unfortunately you will never know the joy of the Christmas season; the cheerfulness that filled all men even those who didn't believe in Christ. The sound of caroling in the streets, the food, clothes, and toys that were given away, the lights and decorations erected, the families gathering around to celebrate and love on one another. How beautiful it was to see the church filled with new faces and happy children ready to present their own production of the birth of Jesus Christ to the public.

The Christmas season was the one time of the year where the church didn't have to go looking for people because the people came and sought the church. They wanted to know what Christmas was all about. Why were people in such a giving mood? Who is this Jesus we speak of? Even though it was unlikely that Jesus was actually born on December 25th it doesn't change the fact that he was born so we celebrated his birth on this date as we celebrated his birth everyday of the year. It was on this day that we had the world's attention. The religions of the world threw stones at us for honoring our savior calling us pagans but we didn't care because it was our right to celebrate whatever holiday we pleased. They were only upset because this time of the year they were bummed out watching us have so much fun.

America celebrated it holidays April fool's Day, St. Patrick's Day, Valentine's Day, Halloween, New Years Eve, and we respected their choices. We never protested but when it came to **CHRIST**mas they wanted Christ out simply because they wanted to silence our witness. Christmas was the time of the year when infiltrating the enemy's camp and presenting the gospel of Jesus Christ to souls was at its easiest because people were more inclined to hear. The world had its own traditions of evergreen trees, lights, reindeer, and a fat man in a red suit but in the midst of those traditions families would gather to hear the story of the birth of Christ. Organizations formed all over the globe in outrage that we were having so much fun this time of year. People would begin to put up billboards, advertisements, and even boycotted stores to have this holiday removed. Obviously they succeeded but only in removing the commercial element of Christmas from the world. They can never stop us from telling the world that man can't work his way up to God but God came down to us and his name is Jesus.

Over 2000 years ago Jesus was born and hundreds of years before he was born men by the revelation of God foretold his coming in complex detail. You would only think that such bold predictions would convince man that God was real. But, once again doubt was cast and the minds of men were too blind to see the obvious. Jesus Christ separates Christianity from all other religions and because of Christ there can't be any comparison to what we believe and what others believe. God himself came down to earth and lived among men as a man and that has caused a huge stumbling block to the world because they can't even entertain such thinking.

The word of God boldly tells the future in great detail. The word of God is 100% accurate which means not one prediction of our Bible has ever failed. The prophet Isaiah hundreds of years before our

Savior came wrote these words *"Therefore the Lord himself shall give you a sign; Behold, a virgin shall conceive, and bear a son, and shall call his name Immanuel. For unto us a child is born, unto us a son is given: and the government shall be upon his shoulder: and his name shall be called Wonderful, Counselor, The mighty God, The everlasting Father, The Prince of Peace."*

Centuries later this is exactly what happened a virgin by the name of Mary from the very bloodline of David the king of Israel would be visited by the angel of the Lord Gabriel who would tell her this "Rejoice, highly favored *one,* the Lord *is* with you; blessed *are* you among women! But when she saw *him,* she was troubled at his saying, and considered what manner of greeting this was. Then the angel said to her, "Do not be afraid, Mary, for you have found favor with God. And behold, you will conceive in your womb and bring forth a Son, and shall call His name JESUS. He will be great, and will be called the Son of the Highest; and the Lord God will give Him the throne of His father David. And He will reign over the house of Jacob forever, and of His kingdom there will be no end." Then Mary said to the angel, "How can this be, since I do not know a man?" And the angel answered and said to her, "*The* Holy Spirit will come upon you, and the power of the Highest will overshadow you; therefore, also, that Holy One who is to be born will be called the Son of God."

Mary was engaged at the time to a carpenter by the name of Joseph who was also of the bloodline of King David and in those days it was frowned upon even punishable by law to engage in sexual activity outside of marriage. Joseph hadn't engaged in sexual activity with Mary and because of that there was a great burden placed on the heart of Joseph because his fiancé was pregnant and he wasn't the father. As a man I'm not sure even what I would've done in Joseph's situation but Joseph was a far more righteous man than any man that I have known. I suppose that's why he was chosen to be the stepfather of our Savior.

Now the birth of Jesus Christ was as follows: After His mother Mary was betrothed to Joseph, before they came together, she was found with child of the Holy Spirit. Then Joseph her husband, being a just *man,* and not wanting to make her a public example, was minded to put her away secretly. But while he thought about these things, behold, an angel of the Lord appeared to him in a dream, saying, "Joseph, son of David, do not be afraid to take to you Mary your wife, for that which is conceived in her is of the Holy Spirit. And she will bring forth a Son, and you shall call His name JESUS, for He will save His people from their sins." So all this was done that it might be fulfilled which was spoken by the Lord through the prophet, saying: *"Behold, the virgin shall be with child, and bear a Son, and they shall call His name Immanuel,"* which is translated, "God with us." Then Joseph, being aroused from sleep, did as the angel of the Lord commanded him and took to him his wife, and did not know her till she had brought forth her firstborn Son. And he called His name JESUS.

A miracle was happening in the lives of Mary and Joseph and because God was using their lives the enemy created conflict. The life of a child of God is one filled with opposition and if anyone tells you that going on a mission for God is easy and void of conflict they have not known what a true mission for God is. Our God had not been a man who reached the level of God but our God became a man and not just a man a fetus in the womb of a woman and this is incomprehensible even in my own understanding but nothing is impossible for God. God became a defenseless weak baby who fed from his mother's breast and had his cloth changed after he soiled himself. Our God crawled on the floor until he had to learn how to walk our God was a child who only knew to depend on his parents and his Father in Heaven for everything. We must understand that we are all babies in the eyes of a God, because God was alive before time existed and we must depend on the Father for all things just as Jesus did. Jesus was despised and rejected of men his very mother was mocked and his step father ridiculed. His mother was accused of being impure and defiled sexually before marriage and his father was mocked because he married a pregnant bride whom he had not been intimate with. The word of God declares:

"And it came to pass in those days *that* a decree went out from Caesar Augustus that all the world should be registered. This census first took place while Quirinius was governing Syria. So all went to be registered, everyone to his own city. Joseph also went up from Galilee, out of the city of Nazareth, into Judea, to the city of David, which is called Bethlehem, because he was of the house and lineage of David, to be registered with Mary, his betrothed wife, who was with child So it was, that while they were there, the days were completed for her to be delivered. And she brought forth her firstborn

Son, and wrapped Him in swaddling cloths, and laid Him in a manger, because there was no room for them in the inn. Now there were in the same country shepherds living out in the fields, keeping watch over their flock by night. And behold, an angel of the Lord stood before them, and the glory of the Lord shone around them, and they were greatly afraid. Then the angel said to them, "Do not be afraid, for behold, I bring you good tidings of great joy which will be to all people. For there is born to you this day in the city of David a Savior, who is Christ the Lord. And this *will be* the sign to you: You will find a Babe wrapped in swaddling cloths, lying in a manger." And suddenly there was with the angel a multitude of the heavenly host praising God and saying: "Glory to God in the highest, And on earth peace, goodwill toward men!" So it was, when the angels had gone away from them into heaven, that the shepherds said to one another, "Let us now go to Bethlehem and see this thing that has come to pass, which the Lord has made known to us." And they came with haste and found Mary and Joseph, and the Babe lying in a manger. Now when they had seen *Him,* they made widely known the saying which was told them concerning this Child. And all those who heard *it* marveled at those things which were told them by the shepherds. But Mary kept all these things and pondered *them* in her heart. Then the shepherds returned, glorifying and praising God for all the things that they had heard and seen, as it was told them."

The wonderful praise that the angels of Heaven sung and the glory and worship that man had given to the young child because they recognized that he is God. The enemies of God were upset at the coming of the Messiah and they would stop at nothing to destroy the young child and much blood was shed as a result.

Now after Jesus was born in Bethlehem of Judea in the days of Herod the king, behold, wise men from the East came to Jerusalem, saying, "Where is He who has been born King of the Jews? For we have seen His star in the East and have come to worship Him." When Herod the king heard *this,* he was troubled, and all Jerusalem with him. And when he had gathered all the chief priests and scribes of the people together, he inquired of them where the Christ was to be born. So they said to him, "In Bethlehem of Judea, for thus it is written by the prophet: *"But you, Bethlehem, in the land of Judah, Are not the least among the rulers of Judah; For out of you shall come a Ruler Who will shepherd My people Israel."* Then Herod, when he had secretly called the wise men, determined from them what time the star appeared. And he sent them to Bethlehem and said, "Go and search carefully for the young Child, and when you have found *Him,* bring back word to me, that I may come and worship Him also." When they heard the king, they departed; and behold, the star which they had seen in the East went before them, till it came and stood over where the young Child was. When they saw the star, they rejoiced with exceedingly great joy. And when they had come into the house, they saw the young Child with Mary His mother, and fell down and worshiped Him. And when they had opened their treasures, they presented gifts to Him: gold, frankincense, and myrrh. Then, being divinely warned in a dream that they should not return to Herod, they departed for their own country another way. Now when they had departed, behold, an angel of the Lord appeared to Joseph in a dream, saying, "Arise, take the young Child and His mother, flee to Egypt, and stay there until I bring you word; for Herod will seek the young Child to destroy Him." When he arose, he took the young Child and His mother by night and departed for Egypt, and was there until the death of Herod, that it might be fulfilled which was spoken by the

Lord through the prophet, saying, *"Out of Egypt I called My Son."* Then Herod, when he saw that he was deceived by the wise men, was exceedingly angry; and he sent forth and put to death all the male children who were in Bethlehem and in all its districts, from two years old and under, according to the time which he had determined from the wise men."

Herod was horrible but he wasn't the first nor the last of the evil men that would persecute the children of God. When I consider the death of those innocent babies and the tears of their parents it makes me never take for granted the Salvation that was given to me by Jesus Christ. We are blessed my children and hopefully you will join the family of God and experience the joy first hand. My chains are but a small thing to suffer for my God and I hold my head up with honor because who shall separate us from the love of Christ? shall tribulation, or distress, or persecution, or famine, or nakedness, or peril, or sword? As it is written, For thy sake we are killed all the day long; we are accounted as sheep for the slaughter. Nay, in all these things we are more than conquerors through him that loved us. For I am persuaded, that neither death, nor life, nor angels, nor principalities, nor powers, nor things present, nor things to come, Nor height, nor depth, nor any other creature, shall be able to separate us from the love of God, which is in Christ Jesus our Lord. My children my love is with you but the love of God shall be with you forever and ever just as it was with Mary and Joseph as they journeyed from Israel to Egypt and back to Israel again on a mission for God as he brought Salvation to a dying world. This is the reason why those organizations fought so hard to have this day erased off the calendar because even all the traditions of men couldn't overshadow the greatest true story to ever be told and that is the coming of our Lord and Savior Jesus Christ. My prayer children is that your hearts are changed forever by these words.

Sincerely,

Adam

Who is Jesus?

Neither is there salvation in any other: for there is none other name under heaven given among men, whereby we must be saved.-Acts 4:12

To my Sons and Daughters,

The cup of my anger overflows and for one moment I wish that I could escape these prison walls and correct the error of the words that fall from your father's tongue like poison. Your father was raised to love the Lord but the events that transpired in his life has caused him to forget this. I pray that one day your father will forgive me for leaving him and that he realizes I only preached the gospel because I love your father and care for his eternal security. I can't lie when your grandmother told me how your father disrespected the very name of Christ and called me a lunatic I was hurt and outraged. Deep down inside your father knows the truth that Jesus is the Messiah and if he believed his own lies you would've never been allowed to return back to your grandmother's home. Your father tells you that Jesus is a figment of my imagination but if that is true then the historical records of Rome, Israel and its citizens that were alive during the time of Christ must all be stricken from the record. If Jesus is a figment of my imagination then the very tomb that he was laid in when he died; that presently is displayed in Israel for the world to see must be removed from the face of the earth. If Jesus is a figment of my imagination then the eyes of the thousands of people who both loved him and hated him who were eyewitnesses to His existence must be told that what they saw was a mirage. If Jesus was a figment of my imagination then tell the eleven men who loved him and died for him without changing their testimony of him.

Jesus himself asked his followers one day "Who do men say I am? When Jesus came into the coasts of Caesarea Philippi, he asked his disciples, saying, Whom do men say that I the Son of man am? And they said, Some say that thou art John the Baptist: some, Elias; and others, Jeremias, or one of the prophets. He saith unto them, But whom say ye that I am? And Simon Peter answered and said, Thou art the Christ, the Son of the living God. And Jesus answered and said unto him, Blessed art thou, Simon Barjona: for flesh and blood hath not revealed it unto thee, but my Father which is in heaven."

God the father has revealed unto men that Jesus is the Christ the Son of the Living God so it doesn't matter who your father, the world, or satan says Jesus is because God already told us the truth. The devil has spread his seeds of doubt throughout the world because he hates for men to worship Christ. The devil told some men that Jesus is a good moral teacher, a great prophet, a man that we should all strive to be but nonetheless he was just a man and not the Savior of the world. Jesus himself said "I am the way, the truth, and the life: no man cometh unto the Father, but by me. If ye had known me, ye should have known my Father also: and from henceforth ye know him, and have seen him."

The devil sought to make himself equal with Jesus so he spread the lie that he was the brother of Jesus and that Jesus was nothing more than an angel who was given a specific job to do. The devil even went so far to take away the name of Christ by convincing people that Jesus is really Michael the Archangel and not the Son of God. The devil is so deceitful that he has transformed himself into a minister of light appearing to some men in true angelic form and convincing people that his lies were truth from God. We always knew when the devil was at work because his lies never change. He wants to convince the world that Jesus is not God, not the Son of God, not the savior of the world; he claims Jesus is just a man, or an angel, or that he doesn't exist. My children there are some who trouble you and want to pervert the gospel of Christ. But even if we, or an angel from heaven, preach any other gospel to you than what we have preached to you, let him be accursed. As we have said before, so now I say again, if anyone preaches any other gospel to you than what you have received, let him be accursed. For do I now persuade men, or God? Or do I seek to please men? For if I still pleased men, I would not be a bondservant of Christ. But I make known to you, children, that the gospel which was preached by me is not according to man. For I neither received it from man, nor was I taught *it,* but *it came* through the revelation of Jesus Christ.

The devil has tried to convince men that Jesus never really had flesh and blood he was just a spirit that moved from place to place; which is convenient for satan because without flesh and blood then the sacrifice of Christ on the cross is null and void. Jesus didn't come to earth to teach us the Christ consciousness or any other strange doctrine of devils. He came to save us from a dying world and the eternal fire that awaits.

Don't believe the lies of the world that there are many paths that lead to Heaven because there is only one path that leads to Heaven. We must enter by the narrow gate; for wide is the gate and broad is the way that leads to destruction, and there are many who go in by it. The whole world is pointing at Christianity laughing and although many religions claim to be similar in belief to what us Christians believe there are none that believe in the gospel of Jesus Christ except our own. Jesus was, is, and forever will be our God, the Son of God, the second person of the Holy trinity regardless of what anybody chooses to believe. For God so loved the world that He gave His only begotten Son, that whoever believes in Him should not perish but have everlasting life.

God created men and men begat other men. God created animals and animals begat other animals. God never created Jesus because that would imply that Jesus is less than him God begat Jesus because the Father and the son are equal just as you and I are equal. Jesus is the heir to the throne one in the same with his Father he is the beginning and the end the alpha and the omega that has no beginning and no end. Who else could die for the sins of the world but God? Whose blood could be a sufficient enough sacrifice to satisfy God but his own? Only God could die to save us and set us free and only God can take on the flesh of a man and live a perfect life free from sin. As it is written:

"But now the righteousness of God apart from the law is revealed, being witnessed by the Law and the Prophets, even the righteousness of God, through faith in Jesus Christ, to all and on all who believe. For there is no difference; for all have sinned and fall short of the glory of God, being justified freely by His grace through the redemption that is in Christ Jesus, whom God set forth *as* a propitiation by His blood, through faith, to demonstrate His righteousness, because in His forbearance God had passed over the sins that were previously committed, to demonstrate at the present time His righteousness, that He might be just and the justifier of the one who has faith in Jesus."-Romans 3:21-26

Mankind through his sin has offended God and separated himself from God. The only way to appease God's anger was to offer a sacrifice for our sins. The problem is that the blood sacrifices men once offered to God were only temporary and could not take away our sins permanently. It is written in the book of Hebrews:

"For the law, having a shadow of the good things to come, and not the very image of the things, can never with these same sacrifices, which they offer continually year by year, make those who approach perfect. For then would they not have ceased to be offered? For the worshipers, once purified, would have had no more consciousness of sins. But in those sacrifices there is a reminder of sins every year. For it is not possible that the blood of bulls and goats could take away sins. Therefore, when He came into the world, He said: "Sacrifice and offering You did not desire, But a body You have prepared for Me. In burnt offerings and sacrifices for sin You had no pleasure. Then I said, 'Behold, I have come In the volume of the book it is written of Me To do Your will, O God.' Previously saying, "Sacrifice and offering, burnt offerings, and offerings for sin You did not desire, nor had pleasure in them " (which are offered according to the law), then He said, "Behold, I have come to do Your will, O God." He takes away the first that He may establish the second. By that will we have been sanctified through the offering of the body of Jesus Christ once for all."

It was the blood of Jesus that appeased the heart of our Father who was offended by the sins of the world. Jesus came to proclaim a message that began like his prophets before him "Repent: for the kingdom of heaven is at hand."

The truth of Jesus saving power is made so clear in his word listen "There was a man of the Pharisees named Nicodemus, a ruler of the Jews. This man came to Jesus by night and said to Him, "Rabbi, we know that You are a teacher come from God; for no one can do these signs that You do unless God is with him." Jesus answered and said to him, "Most assuredly, I say to you, unless one is born again, he cannot see the kingdom of God." Nicodemus said to Him, "How can a man be born when he is old? Can he enter a second time into his mother's womb and be born?" Jesus answered, "Most assuredly, I say to you, unless one is born of water and the Spirit, he cannot enter the kingdom of God. That which is born of the flesh is flesh, and that which is born of the Spirit is spirit. Do not marvel that I said to you, 'You must be born again.' The wind blows where it wishes, and you hear the sound of it, but cannot tell where it comes from and where it goes. So is everyone who is born of the Spirit." Nicodemus answered and said to Him, "How can these things be?" Jesus answered and said to him, "Are you the teacher of Israel, and do not know these things? Most assuredly, I say to you, We speak what We know and testify what We have seen, and you do not receive Our witness. If I have told you earthly things and you do not believe, how will you believe if I tell you heavenly things? No one has ascended to heaven but He who came down from heaven, *that is,* the Son of Man who is in heaven. And as Moses lifted up the serpent in the wilderness, even so must the Son of Man be lifted up, that whoever believes in Him should not perish but have eternal life. For God so loved the world that He gave His only begotten Son, that whoever believes in Him should not perish but have everlasting life. For God did not send His Son into the world to condemn the world, but that the world through Him might be saved. "He who believes in Him is not condemned; but he who does not believe is condemned already, because he has not believed in the name of the only begotten Son of God. And this is the condemnation, that the light has come into the world, and men loved darkness rather than light, because their deeds were evil. For everyone practicing evil hates the light and does not come to the light, lest his deeds should be exposed. But he who does the truth comes to the light, that his deeds may be clearly seen, that they have been done in God."

Jesus made it plain that in order for us to inherit eternal life we must all be born again. My children you were all born once to your mother (God rest her soul) and your father but in order for you to join the family of faith you must be borne by the Spirit of God. In his word it is made plain that "As many that received Jesus, to them gave he power to become the sons of God, even to them that believe on his name: Which were born, not of blood, nor of the will of the flesh, nor of the will of man, but of God."

For years we have endured this claim from the world that we are all children of God but that is a lie. We may have all been created by God because we were placed in the water in our mother's womb and born of the flesh but we were not all born of the Spirit and birthed by the Spirit. I am a child of God because I have been birthed by the Spirit and my prayer is that you will join the family sooner rather than later. The grandfather you have now is much different than the grandfather I used to be, the old me died when the new me began and I have become a new creation and given a new nature. The word of

God testifies "If any man be in Christ, he is a new creature: old things are passed away; behold, all things are become new." My children this is just the beginning of the new life, there is still a change to come even far greater than this but I will hold my tongue and wait patiently for you to ponder these thoughts. I pray that your eyes are opened by the content of this letter and if so then more shall be revealed in due time. Hug your father for me and tell him I love him.

Sincerely,

Adam

Beautiful Ugly

And the LORD God said unto the serpent, Because thou hast done this, thou art cursed above all cattle, and above every beast of the field; upon thy belly shalt thou go, and dust shalt thou eat all the days of thy life: And I will put enmity between thee and the woman, and between thy seed and her seed; it shall bruise thy head, and thou shalt bruise his heel.-Genesis 3:14-15

To my Sons and Daughters,

"To everything there is a season, and a time to every purpose under the heaven: A time to be born, and a time to die; a time to plant, and a time to pluck up that which is planted; A time to kill, and a time to heal; a time to break down, and a time to build up; A time to weep, and a time to laugh; a time to mourn, and a time to dance; A time to cast away stones, and a time to gather stones together; a time to embrace, and a time to refrain from embracing; A time to get, and a time to lose; a time to keep, and a time to cast away; A time to rend, and a time to sew; a time to keep silence, and a time to speak; A time to love, and a time to hate; a time of war, and a time of peace."

God is the creator of time and time is of the utmost importance to God. God has careful laid out plans and a specific timetable for all of his plans to be accomplished because my God is a God of order. My dearest Peter today marks your 18th birthday and from the moment you were born we knew the specific time and date that we would celebrate your 18th birthday. God has his own calendar and has revealed to men the details of his calendar something that all the false gods of the false religions would not attempt for fear of being wrong. Daniel the prophet of our Lord was visited by Gabriel the angel of the Lord and was given insight concerning the times of our Messiah so that the people could prepare for the Messiah much like we have prepared for your birth date today.

"While Daniel was praying the man Gabriel, whom he had seen in the vision at the beginning, being caused to fly swiftly, reached him about the time of the evening offering and he informed *him,* and talked with him, and said, "O Daniel, I have now come forth to give you skill to understand. At the beginning of your supplications the command went out, and I have come to tell *you,* for you *are* greatly beloved; therefore consider the matter, and understand the vision:

"Seventy weeks are determined for your people and for your holy city, to finish the transgression, to make an end of sins, to make reconciliation for iniquity, to bring in everlasting righteousness, to seal up vision and prophecy, and to anoint the Most Holy. *" Know therefore and understand, that from the going forth of the command to restore and build Jerusalem until Messiah the Prince, there shall be seven weeks and sixty-two weeks; The street shall be built again, and the wall, even in troublesome times. "And after the sixty-two weeks Messiah shall be cut off, but not for Himself. "*

Daniel had been given a prophecy concerning the future of the world and the work that God would accomplish in the days to come. God set a timetable of 490 years or 70 periods of 7 years and during that time period he would begin a work and end a work in Israel. During this time the transgression of Israel would be finished, an end of sins would come, reconciliation for their iniquity would be made, everlasting righteousness would be established and the most Holy would be anointed. The timetable would begin when the commandment was given to restore and rebuild the city of Jerusalem and that commandment was given by Artarxes around 445 B.C. to Nehemiah. From the time of the commandment to restore and rebuild

Jerusalem there would be 63 seven year periods to make a total of 483 years and then to the revealing of the Messiah the prince. The Jewish scholars and religious leaders were fully aware of this prophecy and this was a day that they were to be waiting for because God had given them the specific day when Jesus Christ would make his triumphant entry into the city and be worshipped publically as the Messiah.

As the word of God foretold that day came and Jesus entered Jerusalem riding on a Donkey fulfilling the word of God. The prophet Zechariah had told the people of Israel that when this day comes they should *"Rejoice greatly, O daughter of Zion! Shout, O daughter of Jerusalem! Behold, your King is coming to you; He is just and having salvation, Lowly and riding on a donkey, A colt, the foal of a donkey."* Zechariah wrote this hundreds of years before Christ was even born and I can't stress this to you enough that our God is the only God that is bold enough to make detailed prophecies of things to come before they happen with full confidence that he will never be wrong. The people had seen Jesus enter Jerusalem as prophesied:

"And a very great multitude spread their garments in the way; others cut down branches from the trees, and strawed them in the

way. And the multitudes that went before, and that followed, cried, saying, Hosanna to the son of David: Blessed is he that cometh in the name of the Lord; Hosanna in the highest. and when he was come into Jerusalem, all the city was moved, saying, Who is this? And the multitude said, this is Jesus the prophet of Nazareth of Galilee."

The people recognized that day as the day spoken of by the Psalmist hundreds of years before the birth of Christ when he wrote *"The stone which the builders refused is become the head stone of the corner. This is the LORD's doing; it is marvellous in our eyes. This is the day which the LORD hath made; we will rejoice and be glad in it."* This was a beautiful day but the ugly was coming as that prophecy promised that after 483 years the Messiah would be cut off. That's exactly what happened our beautiful savior who for 33 years had walked the earth and opened the eyes of the blind, made the deaf to hear, raised people from the dead, and healed so many of their sickness was cut off from his people in the ugliest way possible.

"Now before the Feast of the Passover, when Jesus knew that His hour had come that He should depart from this world to the Father, having loved His own who were in the world, He loved them to the end. And supper being ended, the devil having already put it into the

heart of Judas Iscariot, Simon's son, to betray Him, Jesus, knowing that the Father had given all things into His hands, and that He had come from God and was going to God, rose from supper and laid aside His garments, took a towel and girded Himself. After that, He poured water into a basin and began to wash the disciples' feet, and to wipe them with the towel with which He was girded. Then He came to Simon Peter. And Peter said to Him, "Lord, are You washing my feet?" Jesus answered and said to him, "What I am doing you do not understand now, but you will know after this." Peter said to Him, "You shall never wash my feet!" Jesus answered him, "If I do not wash you, you have no part with Me." Simon Peter said to Him, "Lord, not my feet only, but also my hands and my head!" Jesus said to him, "He who is bathed needs only to wash his feet, but is completely clean; and you are clean, but not all of you." For He knew who would betray Him; therefore He said, "You are not all clean." So when He had washed their feet, taken His garments, and sat down again, He said to them "Do you know what I have done to you? You call Me Teacher and Lord, and you say well, for so I am. If I then, your Lord and Teacher, have washed your feet, you also ought to wash one another's feet. For I have given you an example, that you should do as I have done to you. Most assuredly, I say to you, a servant is not greater than his master; nor is he who is sent greater than he who sent him. If you know these things, blessed are you if you do them. "I do not speak concerning all of you. I know whom I have chosen; but that the Scripture may be fulfilled, 'He who eats bread with Me has lifted up his heel against Me.' Now I tell you before it comes, that when it does come to pass, you may believe that I am He. Most assuredly, I say to you, he who receives whomever I send receives Me; and he who receives Me receives Him who sent Me." When Jesus had said these things, He was troubled in spirit, and testified and said, "Most assuredly, I say to you, one of you will betray Me." Then the disciples looked at one another, perplexed about whom He spoke. Now there was leaning on Jesus' bosom one of His disciples, whom Jesus loved. Simon Peter therefore motioned to him to ask who it was of whom He spoke. Then, leaning back on Jesus' breast, he said to Him, "Lord, who is it?" Jesus answered, "It is he to whom I shall give a piece of bread when I have dipped it." And having dipped the bread, He gave it to Judas Iscariot, the son of Simon. Now after the piece of bread, Satan entered him. Then Jesus said to him, "What you do, do quickly." But no one at the table knew for what reason He said this to him. For some thought, because Judas had the money box, that Jesus had said to him, "Buy those things we need for the feast," or that he should give something to the poor. Having received the piece of bread, he then went out immediately. And it was night. So, when he had gone out, Jesus said, "Now the Son of Man is glorified, and God is glorified in Him. If God is glorified in Him, God will also glorify Him in Himself, and glorify Him immediately. Little children, I shall be with you a little while longer. You will seek Me; and as I said to the Jews, 'Where I am going, you cannot come,' so now I say to you. A new commandment I give to you, that you love one another; as I have loved you, that you also love one another. By this all will know that you are My disciples, if you have love for one another." Simon Peter said to Him, "Lord, where are You going?" Jesus answered him, "Where I am going you cannot follow Me now, but you shall follow Me afterward." Peter said to Him, "Lord, why can I not follow You now? I will lay down my life for Your sake." Jesus answered him, "Will you lay down your life for My *sake? Most assuredly, I say to you, the rooster shall not crow till you have denied Me three time."*

They called him Judas disciple of Christ, holder of the money bag, friend to Jesus, son of perdition, betrayer of Christ, and murderer of himself. While Jesus was being betrayed by Judas he went to his secret place to pray to his Father:

"When Jesus had spoken these words, he went forth with his disciples over the brook Cedron, where was a garden, into the which he entered, and his disciples. And Judas also, which betrayed him, knew the place: for Jesus ofttimes resorted thither with his disciples. Judas then, having received a band of men and officers from the chief priests and Pharisees, cometh thither with lanterns and torches and weapons. Jesus therefore, knowing all things that should come upon him, went forth, and said unto them, Whom seek ye? They answered him, Jesus of Nazareth. Jesus saith unto them, I am he. And Judas also, which betrayed him, stood with them. As soon then as he had said unto them, I am he, they went backward, and fell to the ground. Then asked he them again, Whom seek ye? And they said, Jesus of Nazareth. Jesus answered, I have told you that I am he: if therefore ye seek me, let these go their way: That the saying might be fulfilled,

which he spake, Of them which thou gavest me have I lost none. Then Simon Peter having a sword drew it, and smote the high priest's servant, and cut off his right ear. The servant's name was Malchus. Then said Jesus unto Peter, Put up thy sword into the sheath: the cup which my Father hath given me, shall I not drink it."

Jesus was betrayed by Judas for 30 pieces of silver and Judas handed over our Lord and betrayed him with a kiss:

"Then Judas, His betrayer, seeing that He had been condemned, was remorseful and brought back the thirty pieces of silver to the chief priests and elders, saying, "I have sinned by betraying innocent blood." And they said, "What is that to us? You see to it!" Then he threw down the pieces of silver in the temple and departed, and went and hanged himself."

Judas was overcome with guilt but not willing to seek forgiveness for his sin and not willing to repent for betraying God and his brothers. Rather than Judas humble himself, confess his sins to the Father, and be reunited with his brothers he chose eternal death. Judas hung himself and fell down a cliff so that his guts fell out of his body. That was the ugly side of a brother's betrayal but Judas wasn't the only disciple to betray Jesus. Peter his faithful disciple would also deny Jesus three times that night but to God be the glory Peter repented of his sins and went back and served Christ for the rest of his life. Jesus was delivered into the hands of the enemies of God by Judas and the ugly would unfold as Jesus was beat until he was unrecognizable. Jesus was blindfolded as men struck him and asked him to prophecy which one of them was hitting him. Jesus had his beard plucked from his face and people spit on Jesus. Jesus was mocked by men, stripped naked and scourged. Hundreds of years before Christ was born the prophet Isaiah told the world this would happen in great detail:

"Who hath believed our report? and to whom is the arm of the LORD revealed? For he shall grow up before him as a tender plant, and as a root out of a dry ground: he hath no form nor comeliness; and when we shall see him, there is no beauty that we should desire him. He is despised and rejected of men; a man of sorrows, and acquainted with grief: and we hid as it were our faces from him; he was despised, and we esteemed him not. Surely he hath borne our griefs, and carried our sorrows: yet we did esteem him stricken, smitten of God, and afflicted. But he was wounded for our

transgressions, he was bruised for our iniquities: the chastisement of our peace was upon him; and with his stripes we are healed. All we like sheep have gone astray; we have turned every one to his own way; and the LORD hath laid on him the iniquity of us all. He was oppressed, and he was afflicted, yet he opened not his mouth: he is brought as a lamb to the slaughter, and as a sheep before her shearers is dumb, so he openeth not his mouth. He was taken from prison and from judgment: and who shall declare his generation? for he was cut off out of the land of the living: for the transgression of my people was he stricken. And he made his grave with the wicked, and with the rich in his death; because he had done no violence, neither was any deceit in his mouth. Yet it pleased the LORD to bruise him; he hath put him to grief: when thou shalt make his soul an offering for sin, he shall see his seed, he shall prolong his days, and the pleasure of the LORD shall prosper in his hand. He shall see of the travail of his soul, and shall be satisfied: by his knowledge shall my righteous servant justify many; for he shall bear their iniquities. Therefore will I divide him a portion with the great, and he shall divide the spoil with the strong; because he hath poured out his soul unto death: and he was numbered with the transgressors; and he bare the sin of many, and made intercession for the transgressors."

Eventually the ugliness in all mankind would be revealed when they took our bloody Savior and nailed his hands and feet to a wooden cross and placed upon his head a crown of thorns. The people watched as Jesus agonized until his death on the cross for the sins of the world past, present, and future:

"Likewise also the chief priests mocking him, with the scribes and elders, said, He saved others; himself he cannot save. If he be the King of Israel, let him now come down from the cross, and we will believe him. He trusted in God; let him deliver him now, if he will have him: for he said, I am the Son of God. The thieves also, which were crucified with him, cast the same in his teeth. Now from the sixth hour there was darkness over all the land unto the ninth hour. And about the ninth hour Jesus cried with a loud voice, saying, Eli, Eli, lama sabachthani? that is to say, My God, my God, why hast thou forsaken me? Some of them that stood there, when they heard that, said, This man calleth for Elias. And straightway one of them ran, and took a spunge, and filled it with vinegar, and put it on a reed, and gave him to drink. The rest said, Let be, let us see whether Elias will

come to save him. Jesus, when he had cried again with a loud voice, yielded up the ghost. And, behold, the veil of the temple was rent in twain from the top to the bottom; and the earth did quake, and the rocks rent; And the graves were opened; and many bodies of the saints which slept arose, And came out of the graves after his resurrection, and went into the holy city, and appeared unto many. Now when the centurion, and they that were with him, watching Jesus, saw the earthquake, and those things that were done, they feared greatly, saying, Truly this was the Son of God. And many women were there beholding afar off, which followed Jesus from Galilee, ministering unto him: Among which was Mary Magdalene, and Mary the mother of James and Joses, and the mother of Zebedees children. When the even was come, there came a rich man of Arimathaea, named Joseph, who also himself was Jesus' disciple: He went to Pilate, and begged the body of Jesus. Then Pilate commanded the body to be delivered. And when Joseph had taken the body, he wrapped it in a clean linen cloth, And laid it in his own new tomb, which he had hewn out in the rock: and he rolled a great stone to the door of the sepulchre, and departed. And there was Mary Magdalene, and the other Mary, sitting over against the sepulchre."

This too my children was also prophesied hundreds of years before my Savior was born even the very words that he spoke from the cross were written in detail by the psalmist:

"My God, my God, why hast thou forsaken me? why art thou so far from helping me, and from the words of my roaring? O my God, I cry in the day time, but thou hearest not; and in the night season, and am not silent. But thou art holy, O thou that inhabitest the praises of Israel. Our fathers trusted in thee: they trusted, and thou didst deliver them. They cried unto thee, and were delivered: they trusted in thee, and were not confounded. But I am a worm, and no man; a reproach of men, and despised of the people. All they that see me laugh me to scorn: they shoot out the lip, they shake the head, saying, He trusted on the LORD that he would deliver him: let him deliver him, seeing he delighted in him."

"They gaped upon me with their mouths, as a ravening and a roaring lion. I am poured out like water, and all my bones are out of joint: my heart is like wax; it is melted in the midst of my bowels. My strength is dried up like a potsherd; and my tongue cleaveth to my

jaws; and thou hast brought me into the dust of death. For dogs have compassed me: the assembly of the wicked have inclosed me: they pierced my hands and my feet. I may tell all my bones: they look and stare upon me. They part my garments among them, and cast lots upon my vesture."

The words could only describe how ugly this was but my children the beautiful would come three days later just as our Messiah prophesied:

"Now the next day, that followed the day of the preparation, the chief priests and Pharisees came together unto Pilate, Saying, Sir, we remember that that deceiver said, while he was yet alive, After three days I will rise again. Command therefore that the sepulchre be made sure until the third day, lest his disciples come by night, and steal him away, and say unto the people, He is risen from the dead: so the last error shall be worse than the first. Pilate said unto them, Ye have a watch: go your way, make it as sure as ye can. So they went, and made the sepulchre sure, sealing the stone, and setting a watch.

In the end of the sabbath, as it began to dawn toward the first day of the week, came Mary Magdalene and the other Mary to see the sepulchre. And, behold, there was a great earthquake: for the angel of the Lord descended from heaven, and came and rolled back the stone from the door, and sat upon it. His countenance was like lightning, and his raiment white as snow: And for fear of him the keepers did shake, and became as dead men. And the angel answered and said unto the women, Fear not ye: for I know that ye seek Jesus, which was crucified. He is not here: for he is risen, as he said. Come, see the place where the Lord lay. And go quickly, and tell his disciples that he is risen from the dead; and, behold, he goeth before you into Galilee; there shall ye see him: lo, I have told you. And they departed quickly from the sepulchre with fear and great joy; and did run to bring his disciples word. And as they went to tell his disciples, behold, Jesus met them, saying, All hail. And they came and held him by the feet, and worshipped him. Then said Jesus unto them, Be not afraid: go tell my brethren that they go into Galilee, and there shall they see me."

The day was ugly because Jesus died for our sins; but beautiful because the Blood of Jesus Christ cleanses us from all sin. Jesus died for the sins of the world; my sins your sins all of our sins and it was an ugly death but a beautiful gift to understand that God commendeth his love toward us, in that, while we were yet sinners, Christ died for us. The grace of God cost Jesus so much that none of us could ever consider it cheap nor could any of us take it for granted. You ask me why I smile while I sit in these chains it's because Jesus asked me to embrace these chains and considering what Jesus has done for me it is but a small thing for me to do what Jesus has asked me to do. The truth is even though I sit in these chains it is Jesus that sits with me and gives me strength because Jesus knows that I couldn't endure one day of this prison without Him.

When I sit in my cell at night reading my Bible that I have hidden from the prison guards I'm encouraged by the testimony of my brothers before me who stood before their persecutors and were asked *"Did we not strictly command you not to teach in this name? And look, you have filled Jerusalem with your doctrine, and intend to bring this Man's blood on us!" With great boldness they said "We ought to obey God rather than men. The God of our fathers raised up Jesus whom you murdered by hanging on a tree. Him God has exalted to His right hand to be Prince and Savior, to give repentance to Israel and forgiveness of sins. And we are His witnesses to these things, and so also is the Holy Spirit whom God has given to those who obey Him."*

This is the Jesus we preach my children and its nothing more that I can say or reveal to you other than what has already been told. The beautiful ugly is that God spoke this whole world into existence but to save me God had to bleed.

Sincerely,

Adam

The Call

For God so loved the world, that he gave his only begotten Son, that whosoever believeth in him should not perish, but have everlasting life.-John 3:16

Time to Answer

Again, he limiteth a certain day, saying in David, To day, after so long a time; as it is said, To day if ye will hear his voice, harden not your hearts.-Hebrews 4:17

To my Sons and Daughters,

The day is far spent and the sunset is almost upon us. I must tend to my Father's business while it is yet day because when the night falls I won't have an opportunity to work. You were created and you have a maker and we call that maker God. Do you understand that this world is awesome and it didn't just come to be but it was intelligently designed by that same God? Billions of snowflakes have fallen but yet there will never be two snowflakes that are alike. Search all over the world and throughout time and understand that nobody has been created exactly like you. Look at your hands and fingerprints and understand they are 100% yours nobody else in this world will have your fingerprints. Did you know that humans inhale oxygen given to us by trees and we exhale carbon dioxide which goes back into the trees and comes back to us in the form of oxygen? Did you know that when we are sleeping our brain continues to keep us breathing even though we are not trying? Have you ever tried to make your heart stop beating? The answer is you can't the heart is simply controlled you couldn't stop it if you wanted to.

We are not here by mistake the earth didn't just happen to be in perfect position to sustain life. We are here for a purpose and only God knows what that purpose is. I write these letters to you in hopes that you will be inspired to seek a personal relationship with God. There comes a time in a person's life where they must seek the truth about their existence and the meaning of life. Many waste a whole lifetime going on a quest for hidden knowledge, conspiracies, and the creations of the human imagination only to die more confused than they first started. I'm here to tell you the truth is right in our face and there is a loving God who would never hide himself from his creation. This same loving God has revealed himself openly from the beginning of time because he has always wanted a relationship with his creation. The truth has been made plain for all mankind to see, yet people ignore the truth for their own personal achievement. They exchange the truth for hard labor and they afflict themselves. They create impossible rules for themselves and then change them over and over again. Even though they become miserable because they can't live up to their own standards; they still choose to teach others to live like them.

The truth has been declared in the word of God as it says "He who does not love does not know God, for God is love. In this the love of God was manifested toward us, that God has sent His only begotten Son into the world, that we might live through Him. In this is love, not that we loved God, but that He loved us and sent His Son *to be* the propitiation for our sins."

What is truth? Truth is that God loves us all and because he loves us so much he died for us. Before the world began God promised us eternal life and our God cannot lie. The devil has the world confused believing that somehow that if they work hard enough their good works will somehow outweigh their bad works one day. Suppose hypothetically a man committed just one sin a day over the course of a year that would accumulate to 365 sins a year. Suppose that same man lived to be 60 years old and over the course of 60 years if that man kept a pace of one sin a day that total would equal 21,900 sins over a lifetime. It is impossible for a person to be that good because we are sinful creatures who all commit more than one sin a day whether it is physically, spiritually, or mentally. The devil has convinced some that committing suicide for religious purposes guarantees them a place in heaven. There are others who have been hoodwinked into believing the cruelest lie of them all that somehow they will die and be reincarnated forced to live in this cruel world over and over again until they get it right. These are the lies of satan and the fairytales of imagination upon death we will not cease to exist every soul will live the question is where. The truth has been written and it is this:

"Whoever believes that Jesus is the Christ is born of God, and everyone who loves Him who begot also loves him who is begotten of Him. By this we know that we love the children of God, when we love God and keep His commandments. For this is the love of God, that we keep His commandments. And His commandments are not burdensome. For whatever is born of God overcomes the world. And this is the victory that has overcome the world—our faith. Who is he who overcomes the world, but he who believes that Jesus is the Son of God? This is He who came by water and blood—Jesus Christ; not only by water, but by water and blood. And it is the Spirit who bears witness, because the Spirit is truth. For there are three that bear witness in heaven: the Father, the Word, and the Holy Spirit; and these three are one. And there are three that bear witness on earth: the Spirit, the water, and the blood; and these three agree as one. If we receive the witness of men, the witness of God is greater; for this is the witness of God which He has testified of His Son. He who believes in the Son of God has the witness in himself; he who does not believe God has made Him a liar, because he has not believed the testimony that God has given of His Son. And this is the testimony: that God has given us eternal life, and this life is in His Son. He who has the Son has life; he who does not have the Son of God does not have life. These things I have written to you who believe in the name of the Son of God, that you may know that you have eternal life-and that you may *continue to* believe in the name of the Son of God."

The very Bible was written that all men may know the truth and the truth is that God guarantees eternal life to all who put their trust in him and his testimony. I know for sure now what I didn't know laying in my hospital bed many years ago. Your grandmother asked me "If I were to die today would I be sure that I had eternal life? If I was to stand before God and he asked why should I let you into Heaven what answer would I give him?" Many years ago those questions brought me to tears and today nothing has changed but I cry tears of joy now because I know the answer. I know for sure that if I died today I'm going to heaven and not because I been a good boy but because Jesus died for my sins. I pray that you realize that God has better things for us and a better place for us. He has established a place where he dwells and we can know for sure that if we were to die today that we shall be there with him guaranteed.

Imagine a place where all tears will be wiped away and there will be no need for crying. Imagine a place where sorrow, pain and sickness are long forgotten. Imagine a place where death doesn't exist but we live forever in bodies that words can't describe. Imagine a place prepared just for you by the creator himself and you never have to leave. Imagine a place where expensive stones such as pearls, onyx, and sapphires are used as building material and gold is used to pave the streets because those things have no value. Imagine being able to buy food and clothes without using money. Imagine living for eternity with the creator of the whole universe and never getting bored. The place I am referring to is heaven and the cost is free. The paradise that our creator has given to us can't be earned or deserved but it is given to us as a free gift from him.

How in the world can a place so breathtaking that words can't describe be given to us for free? Many people ask themselves that question rather than just take the greatest deal ever offered. The false religions of the world all agree that a man must work for their salvation and our Jesus tells us that he has already completed the work on the cross. If a person worked their way up to heaven wouldn't that imply that God somehow owed them or was in debt to them? That's ridiculous because what could God who created all things ever owe a man. Could you imagine the ruckus in heaven of men standing before God saying "God I finished my course now pay me the Heaven that you owe me." The bible itself makes this clear to us in the book of Romans 4: 4-5 "When people work, their wages are not a gift, but something they have earned. But people are counted as righteous, not because of their work, but because of their faith in God who forgives sinners." Could you imagine the ruckus in heaven of the many men bragging about how much work they got done on earth and their salvation was greater than others because they worked so much harder?

Yet again the word of God makes it very clear in Ephesians 2:8 "For by grace you have been saved through faith, and that not of yourselves; *it is* the gift of God, not of works, lest anyone should boast." When a parent has a child if that child is hungry the parent doesn't make that child work for food but will feed their child because of love for that child. If a parent has a child that is approaching a dangerous situation that parent issues a warning out of love. If a parent observes a child in immediate danger that parent will rescue that child the minute that parent is aware of that danger. A good parent will always want the best for their child. That's who God is to us he is our Father. A Father that loves you more than any words can describe. Our Father God has given his children the gift of eternal life in heaven with him. How is this possible? It is possible because our Father has recognized that we are bad people and not good people. We are guilty before his eyes because he desires us to be like him and he is perfect and holy. When children make mistakes and mess up correction is needed. When children are rebellious and disobedient willfully then punishment is in order. Our Father in heaven is no different. Human beings have messed up we lie, cheat, steal, and commit horrible acts before other people and God.

Has your father ever given you instructions and you got upset and had thoughts in your head that you couldn't say out loud or perform? Our Father even knows our thoughts and he takes those into his record book as well. We are certainly guilty before Almighty God because he is perfect and his standard of judgment is perfection and we aren't perfect. Since we are guilty we can't go to heaven until we have been made free or justified. We can't work our way up to God because God had a plan to come down to us which he carried out in his Son. God has a Son, and not just a Son but a Son who is God just like he is. God the father has a Son who came down from heaven and left the presence of his father to live with mankind. He gave mankind the truth because he is the truth and he has set mankind free. One day we will all stand before God and give an account for the life we have lived and we will all be guilty before God. The word of God declares that God will not clear the guilty but God has made provision based on the fact that he loves us and that provision is salvation. God looked upon man and realized that he would take the punishment for mankind and sent Jesus Christ to die on the cross for our sins. We did wrong and Jesus accepted the call for our redemption and paid the price so we can go to heaven for free. The beautiful place with the gold streets is ours because God was willing to sacrifice his only begotten son in our place. Jesus died on the cross for our sins and he rose from the dead so that he could defeat death for us. True we will die on earth but we have the option to live forever with the father in heaven or to go to the place of eternal damnation.

How can I make this choice? It is simple confess that Jesus Christ is the son of God and believe in your heart that he died for your sins, and believe God rose him from the dead and you shall have eternal life guaranteed. Really trust Jesus Christ alone for your salvation. Commit to Jesus and follow his instructions through life found in his word to us the Holy Bible. Imagine that you were drowning in an ocean yet there was a lifeguard there willing to save you. The lifeguard extends his hand unto you and asks you to grab his hand. If you grab the lifeguards hand then you will be saved but if you reject the lifeguards hand you will drown. Jesus is our lifeguard and in his hand is salvation from death. Will you receive his salvation or reject it and drown in your own sin? Hopefully you will choose to accept his hand and once you do you will appreciate the wonderful gift that has been given to you. A gift that was absolutely free don't you want to go and tell the world about this gift? When we discover this free gift for ourselves we should desire to share it with everyone so we tell them about Jesus. We live a life according to what we believe in and who we believe in.

Imagine going to a restaurant for the first time and the waiter brings you a menu. You get excited and then you ask the waiter "How does the food taste?" The waiter replies "I don't know because I never eat here." That is how we as believers look when we don't live according to the word of God. We may recommend salvation to others but we ourselves haven't tried anything in the bible out for ourselves. Good works are not necessary for salvation but are definitely necessary for us to be a witness of that salvation. Do you see the difference now? Our Father wants a relationship with us and this relationship is made possible when we trust in Jesus Christ and commit our lives to him. Imagine God whom the bible declares that his right hand spans the entire universe calling you son or daughter yet that is exactly what is happening in the lives of people all over the world as we speak. God wants to fellowship with you and that is made possible by believing that his son paid the price for you on the cross and that there is no other way to God but by Jesus Christ. That is true faith and that is the call that God has desired for all of us. He has called us to live with him will you answer?

Sincerely,

Adam

Power to the People

But ye shall receive power, after that the Holy Ghost is come

upon you: and ye shall be witnesses unto me both in Jerusalem, and

in all Judaea, and in Samaria, and unto the uttermost part of the

earth.-Acts 1:8

To my Sons and Daughters,

Jesus said there is joy in Heaven over one sinner that repents and I say unto you there is much joy in Heaven now. I'm so excited over you my children because you have repented for your sins. My heart is filled with passion and joy yet filled with tears because your father and your brother Mark have rejected the faith. This is a beautiful ugly but we must not cease praying for your brother and father in hopes that they will see the light. I remember when I first fell in love with Jesus there wasn't a miraculous feeling that I felt but there was a new trust that I had in my heart. There was a confidence that I had in Christ that my life was safe in Jesus and I could trust Jesus to guide my every step. My heart belonged to Christ and my every desire turned from pleasing myself to pleasing Him with each moment. For the first time in my life the veil of doubt had been removed and the word of God was revealed unto me and I began not only reading the word but understanding the word of God. I began to apply the word of God to my life and the more truth that was revealed to me the more I realized how far from perfection I really was. I would begin each day in prayer asking God to fix my faults and use my life for his glory.

Metaphorically speaking Jesus was like a dentist and I had walked into his dentist office because I had a toothache. Soon I would discover that the toothache was the least of my problems. Jesus promised to perfect all of our lives as he said "Therefore you shall be perfect, just as your Father in heaven is perfect." My life was changing I carried around a pocket size Bible, I prayed all the time, even the radio station in my car had changed from a music station to a station that preached the gospel 24hrs a day. Church became a second home for me and I longed each day for fellowship with the body of Christ. My faith really became active when me and your Uncle Benjamin would walk the streets and share the gospel of Jesus Christ with others. We got spit on, cursed at, beat up, doors slammed in our face, and even had our lives threatened for trying to share our faith. Those were the good ole days. We were so frustrated in the beginning because we expected everyone we shared the gospel with to say yes but of course this didn't happen.

My grandfather was a wise man and he noticed our frustration so one day he pulled us to the side and had a talk with us "I'm glad that you two are members of the body of Christ and are willing to go out and witness Christ to the world but why do you guys look so frustrated?" We didn't want to tell grandpa that we were having a hard time witnessing for fear that he would be disappointed in us so we both just stared at him with a blank stare. We were so young in the faith but I thank God we had a grandfather that understood our mentality. "Listen boys, the message that you deliver to people is God's message and the power of that message is God's. The message that you are delivering comes from God and the person hearing the message must respond to God and not you. You two are just instruments used by God to share his message. God doesn't need you to deliver his message to people but he loves to include you because it helps build your faith. Take the pressure off of yourselves it's God that is at work just be available and keep sharing his word. Some people plant the seeds and others water the seed and God gives the increase and eventually the plant is ready to harvest.

For years people witnessed the gospel to me and I never responded but one day it all made sense. Every single person that witnessed the gospel to me played a part in me coming to Christ. This is a team effort we study our word to be prepared to share, we pray for divine appointments, and then we share the faith and leave the results in God's hands. What I'm certain of is that one of four things can occur when you share the faith. The first is that the seed will fall by the wayside and the fowls of the air will come and devour it up. That means that when the gospel is shared some people will hear it but satan will come and immediately take the word that was sown into their hearts away from them. When this happens a person is left with no chance for the word to grow in them. The second possibility is that the seed which is the word of God will fall on stony ground where there isn't much earth and it will immediately grow but when the sun comes out it will burn the plant because it doesn't have a root and the plant withers away. There are some that will hear the word of God and receive it with gladness but because the word was not rooted in them when hard times arise such as affliction or persecution they get offended and quit.

Young men I have lost many close friends in the faith that I thought were true Christians. Some even Pastors and missionaries that walked away from the faith because of hard times, the threat of imprisonment, lawsuits, and death. Some even dared to walk away because they had questions about suffering that couldn't be answered. Others walked away because of their own lust and I tell you the truth they were never saved. They were only surface Christians who served some 2 months and others almost 50 years before the sun rose and scorched them. The next possibility is some fell among thorns and the thorns grew up and choked the plant and they never yielded fruit. These people heard the word but the cares of this world and the deceitfulness of riches and the lust of other things entered in and choked the word. The witness of the gospel was destroyed in their life and the plant never bared fruit. It is hurtful thing to see people that say I love God but they give their life to the desires of this world. They have a heart full of their own desires and they never had any intention of giving up their desires to take on Christ desires. They never picked up their cross and followed after him and they were only professors of the faith but not doers.

The final possibility is that the seed will fall on good ground and it will produce much fruit that sprang up and increased and brought forth some thirty, and some sixty, and some hundred. These are those who are sown on good ground they hear the word of God and receive it and bring forth some thirtyfold, some sixty, and some a hundred. When a person heart is opened and the word of God is planted into that heart the heart will take the whole word of God and allow their lives to be governed by the word of God. The work of God will overtake their life and results will begin to happen. My children, my heart is overjoyed that you are concerned about the results because at least you want to see something happen in and through your life for Christ.

A person can only gain a heart like this from the Holy Spirit and it is the Holy Spirit working in you that wants to genuinely see others get saved. Not everyone has a heart like this some only want to brag and boast about how many they were able to bring to the Lord. I tell you that is the work of pride and although they may lead some to Christ their own soul is the one that needs the help. I worked hard for

Christ but I never worked for my salvation. I was committed to sharing the gospel of Jesus Christ with others. Go out young men and be bold for Christ, put a smile on your face, and have fun because a Christian hasn't lived until they have shared their faith." Looking back that conversation changed our lives we hit the streets with reckless abandon only looking to get the message out and years later here I am still sharing.

There is a guard that works here when he was younger he treated me very harshly but over the years he has become like a son to me. His name is Timothy and he is the reason why I am able to mail these letters to you without facing serious punishment. Timothy has been on fire for Jesus for many years every since his wife was healed from stomach cancer. Timothy came to me late one night and asked me to pray for his sick wife and to God be the glory she was healed. Timothy has founded a church that he operates on early Friday mornings just before the sun comes up in the old abandoned dairy farms in the inland empire. Your grandmother has been attending his church since I first started mailing these letters and I want you to start going with her. Timothy has Bibles that he has received from our brothers in Mexico and he will disciple you in the faith. There are many other believers there from all age ranges. I believe the church has over 500 underground members and growing daily. So far we have been able to avoid being shut down and I ask that you begin praying that we can continue assembling. I am leery about you taking Mark to church with you since he is not a believer but I am hopeful that going to the church will help him come to the faith. Pray my children!

Sincerely,

Adam

The Coming

Which also said, Ye men of Galilee, why stand ye gazing up into heaven? this same Jesus, which is taken up from you into heaven, shall so come in like manner as ye have seen him go into heaven.-Acts 1:11

Neglected Love

Nevertheless I have somewhat against thee, because thou hast left

thy first love. Remember therefore from whence thou art fallen, and

repent, and do the first works; or else I will come unto thee quickly,

and will remove thy candlestick out of his place, except thou repent. –

Revelation 2:4-5

To my Sons and Daughters,

The Apostle Paul under the inspiration of the Holy Spirit wrote "Who shall separate us from the love of Christ? Shall tribulation, or distress, or persecution, or famine, or nakedness, or peril, or sword? As it is written: "For Your sake we are killed all day long; We are accounted as sheep for the slaughter." Yet in all these things we are more than conquerors through Him who loved us. For I am persuaded that neither death nor life, nor angels nor principalities nor powers, nor things present nor things to come, nor height nor depth, nor any other created thing, shall be able to separate us from the love of God which is in Christ Jesus our Lord."

Jesus really loves us and he loves us with more love than any human being could ever love us with. Jesus watches over us as a husband does over his bride. Jesus cares for us and he makes us shine like bright stars. His very presence in our lives illuminates through us bringing light to a dark world. Jesus watches over us perfecting us and when we make mistakes he corrects us. The word of God has made it clear that this relationship we have with Christ can never be lost but consider this word of warning it can be neglected or left. Jesus once said concerning us "My sheep hear my voice, and I know them, and they follow me: And I give unto them eternal life; and they shall never perish, neither shall any man pluck them out of my hand. My Father, which gave them me, is greater than all; and no man is able to pluck them out of my Father's hand. I and my Father are one." Listen, my dear children I challenge you to exercise patience with your brethren because we are all imperfect creatures. I challenge you to pray always and never give up."

I challenge you to endure the trials and the attacks that come upon you because of your faith in Christ. Allow God to be your strength. I challenge you to fellowship with other believers and experience the joy and sorrow of being believers together as a family. I challenge you to worship privately and collectively because we all serve the same Lord. There will be ups and there will be downs but don't let the frustration consume you. There will be some that walk amongst us and pretend to be our brothers and sisters but secretly they're agents of the enemy but don't take it to heart. Jesus had twelve disciples and even one of them betrayed him and as the church grows there is no telling how many Judas's have crept in the fellowship. I challenge you to always pray and seek the Bible concerning church discipline and never sweep things under the rug. I challenge you to serve Christ with all of your heart and never lose the desire to serve him.

I challenge you to be passionate unquenchable worshippers for Christ and I challenge you because I love you. I challenge you to witness to those who don't believe. Witness with great boldness and without fear. I challenge you to study to show thyself approved unto God, a workman that needeth not to be ashamed, rightly dividing the word of truth. I challenge you to warn those who are unruly, comfort the fainthearted, uphold the weak, be patient with all. See that no one renders evil for evil to anyone, but always pursue what is good both for yourselves and for all. Rejoice always, pray without ceasing, in everything give thanks; for this is the will of God in Christ Jesus for you. Do not quench the Spirit. Do not despise prophecies. Test all things; hold fast what is good and abstain from every form of evil.

I challenge you because a long time ago I neglected my first love and that was the most miserable time of my life as a believer. I almost destroyed my own soul and if it had not been for the conviction of the Holy Spirit I might still be wandering aimlessly as a believer who has neglected the love of his husband (Jesus Christ). There came a time in my walk with Christ when my passion for Christ had decreased but my duty for his church had increased. I began to neglect my personal time with God and my personal prayer life had become almost nonexistent. My devotion to God turned from pure love to duty and I stopped fearing what Jesus might think of my actions and start fearing what the church would think of my actions. I was devoted to the church and growing the ministry. I only studied and read my Bible to preach a message and all my personal time became about my own needs. I was an up and comer in the world and I was determined to make my mark on the world as the greatest Christian that ever lived.

Be careful my children the devil will offer a Christian the keys to the world if they just bow down at his feet. On the outside my world looked good the church was growing and the people really trusted me as their leader but I was a failure. I was running the church without the love of Christ and eventually the cancer began to spread throughout the congregation.

My self-righteous attitude became the congregations self righteous attitude. My lack of compassion I had for those who didn't follow Christ became the congregation's lack of compassion for the lost. My lack of personal prayer time became the congregation's lack of personal prayer time. My cancerous ambition eventually became the congregation's cancerous ambition to grow larger and more fabulous. I no longer had the daily desire in my heart to please God instead I rose every morning tired from carrying the burdens of the church. My fellowship with God had diminished and I was clueless as to why I felt this way. After all I attended church regularly, I prayed, I studied my Bible but honestly only because I felt obligated to please the church. The enemy began to bring doubt into my mind. Every now and then thoughts would come into my mind that maybe I was never a believer, or maybe I should consider Islam as being the truth. I was in a state of confusion and my life was in decline.

The things I once considered to be immoral I found myself justifying and using my Christian liberty as an excuse. I was married to Christ but what good is marriage without love, trust, and communication. Ironically it was your father whom God used to open my eyes and show me how far I had slipped. One night before he was going to bed he asked me "How come we never pray together anymore?" My heart broke instantly because it was at that moment that I realized that I had neglected my first love. I prayed with your father that night and I had a long conversation with your grandmother and she laid it all out for me. It was clear to me that since my grandfather died and left me the church I had changed. The joy I once had in serving the Lord was replaced with the desire to be better than my grandfather. I made a critical error in that I forgot that the church belongs to Jesus and that means the problems of the church belong to Christ as well. It was my job to receive instruction from Christ on how to deal with those problems but instead I took those problems on as my own and it was killing me.

I never lost my first love Jesus was always there for me and he never abandoned me. However, I walked away from Christ from a intimate standpoint and I needed to go back. I reflected on my life and I could remember a time when my walk with Christ was stronger than it was currently. I had many stories of the good ole days but few stories of the present days. It was clear I was living in the past instead of the present. I wasn't growing in Christ and the people around me suffered because of it. I needed to return to Christ (humbly) and spend much time in prayer remembering our relationship. I had to repent for my sins and renew my love affair with Christ whole heartedly.

The end of Christians who don't go back to their first love is very bitter, confusing, and dark. It is my desire that your ending with Christ be sweeter than your beginning with Christ. That your passion for Christ increases as your physical days on earth decrease. I look back at those days and the power of God wasn't working in my life. My prayers weren't getting further than my ceiling. I remember praying during that dark time in my life and my prayers were filled with doubt. I knew God could do certain things but I seriously doubted that he would. When your passion for Christ simmers so does your trust in his word.

I challenge you to stay passionate and forever trusting in Christ. I challenge you to never come to place in your spiritual life where Heaven is more important than the creator of Heaven and Earth. Never lose the desire for Christ that you have now it's new and beautiful. Everyday should be new and beautiful when you're walking with Christ. There should never be a dull day or a day when everything seems routine because every day is a brand new day to impact the world for Christ.

Dear Heavenly Father I pray that these children will seek the one who rewards rather than the reward. Hold these children in your hand and comfort them through these difficult days. I ask that their brother Mark will come to the faith and also for their father and my son that he will choose you as well. Let their passion always burn for you and let them never leave their first love. Father if they do leave their first love let them remember, repent, and go back to doing their first works. Be glorified in these children in Jesus name we pray.-Amen

Sincerely,

Adam

Sound Doctrine

Fear none of those things which thou shalt suffer: behold, the devil shall cast some of you into prison, that ye may be tried; and ye shall have tribulation ten days: be thou faithful unto death, and I will give thee a crown of life.-Revelation 2:10

To my Sons and Daughters,

The time has come when they will not endure sound doctrine and after their own lust they have heaped upon themselves teachers, having itching ears; and those teachers have turned their ears from the truth towards fables. There is an evil upon us! Men we once considered brothers have devoted their souls to the cause of the enemy in exchange for power and economic prosperity. My children today we have suffered a great blow. Nothing breaks my heart more than to see Jameson betray the church and betray the Lord Jesus Christ for foolishness. Jameson and I have preached the gospel together all over the world from Thailand to Russia and now he has turned his back on the God he pretended to love. The American government has formed a council of religious leaders from all major religions and together they have created a new religion that will help lead America into the future. America has sold its soul to Babylon and this one nation religion will soon be part of a one world religion; with one leader over them all.

The world around us is changing my children as Jameson and the others have been granted permission by the government to seize all the former church buildings and turn them into the Temples of Semiramis. It is a slap in the face to believers everywhere to see our places of worship defiled by pagan gods. Our former brothers have sold us out for profit and created the perfect condition for Babylon and the New American government to manipulate the people. Jameson offers the people jobs, shelter, food, and clothes if they become members of the Temple and pledge their allegiance to the god of the temple Tammuz.

We must preach the gospel more aggressively than ever because the people are being deceived at a rapid rate and our God is not willing that any should perish, but that all should come to repentance. These are deceptive days but we must continue on in the faith. We have been given the promise land and now is not the time to run back to Egypt because times are difficult. Look to your left and to your right and promise to be your brother's keeper because when the attacks upon us begin some will be tempted to put their trust in the Temple of Semiramis and that will be their downfall. Jameson and all of his lies manipulating the word of God, telling people that Christ is not coming back, preaching to them that we are all Christ and we are all little gods. My stomach is sick to see people deceived by fables listening to the lies of Jameson as he preaches to them stories of the Great White Masters, the lost land of Atlantis, and the power of Aquarius. Each and every day people are flocking to the temple worshipping the statue of Semiramis holding her son Tammuz and burning incense to the great red dragon in hopes of receiving power from it.

They are deceiving the people with parlor tricks and calling them miracles. They are laying empty hands on people and pushing them to the ground and saying look at the power of god. They have encouraged the people to babble foolishly telling them that by chanting certain words they will have the gifts of tongues. They are telling the people to laugh uncontrollable and dance exotically so they can provoke the power of God on their lives. It was all deception many of the people were planted in the Temple by Jameson to deceive the people. Jameson and the other Guru's knew that if they can offer the people things that were familiar to them then they could use those same things to deceive them. The sad part is that human nature causes people to not want to feel left out so pretty soon people began to pretend that the power was real. They are teaching people that the resurrection was a lie and that we must all be reincarnated on this earth and dwell here forever. They are teaching men to pray to the dead for divine protection and lead them in prayers to Abraham, Joseph Smith, L. Ron Hubbard, Mary, Mohammed. The temple had become a well run corporation with Jameson being at the top of the hierarchy; he alone holds the title of Zeus. Under Jameson or Guru Zeus many other men have been appointed as Guru's and some of our brothers and sisters have bowed down to his authority.

They seek to change the cross of Christ from a tool that our savior died on to a holy oracle to be idolized and worshipped. We have an enemy that never sleeps and never takes a day off so we must always be ready for war. In this war a good soldier for Christ must exhibit the same moral character as Christ. We must be ready to give our life for the church as Christ gave his life for the church. We must live as Christ lives and live honest lives before Christ. There must be no secrets between Christ and ourselves we must confess our sins, pray about our doubt, and ask for help with our shortcomings. Jesus wants us to follow his example and we must be in agreement with Christ in order to walk together with Christ. If we live our lives like this the whole church will be on one accord and the attacks of the enemy will fail.

In times such as these there is always the temptation to let your guard down and let your light dim so you can blend in with the crowd. I assure you that is the enemy casting doubt into your mind. *We are a chosen generation, a royal priesthood, a holy nation, a peculiar people and we shall show forth the praises of him who has called us out of darkness into his marvellous light.* We are Disciples of Christ we don't fit in with the world but we are made a spectacle before all men and angels. *My children do not be conformed to this world, but be transformed by the renewing of your mind, that you may prove what is that good and acceptable and perfect will of God. My children let your light so shine before men, that they may see your good works and glorify your Father in heaven.* The enemy should never take us by surprise as I shouldn't have been surprised by Jameson being a wolf in sheep's clothing. The world is sinful, man is sinful, and sin has become the nature of this fallen world. We live a repented life and to the world a life that seeks to be free from sin is unnatural. Jameson and many others have followed the desires of their flesh or human nature while we seek to live according to the spiritual nature of our Lord. Jameson and all the Pastors that have followed him have been consumed by their lust and they are willing to destroy the church to have those things.

The world is our battleground children, the church is our home base and greater guard must be kept over the church. We must identify those who whisper and cause dissension and see that we deal with them properly. This is war my children and the church is under attack. Enemy agents have descended upon us seeking to steal members out of the fellowship by making them promises of a better life. We face great difficulties as members of the church our jobs have been taken, businesses boycotted or burned to the ground, homes destroyed, and we have been forced to live in poverty! We may be poor to the world but we are rich in God and my **God** shall **supply** all your need according to His riches in glory by Christ Jesus! We serve a God that has made food rain from the sky and if need be he will do it again!

Look around my children we have never went a day without, we have real friends to share our lives with, and we have peace. We are not living in poverty it is the world that has been deprived of all of the riches of Christ. We are witnesses that the Bible is real as we see the truth of its pages unfold and the world is blind to the facts. Everyday more souls are being added to the fellowship and more Bibles are being printed. Peter my oldest grandson I want you to pray hard and ask the Lord for guidance because Pastor Timothy and I have a favor to ask of you. The demand for Bibles is rising and we need more people to help us fulfill that need. I want to know if you would be willing to journey with one of our mission teams to Enredira, Mexico to pick up Bibles and bring them back to the United States. This is a difficult task and if you're not called to do this then don't do simply because I'm asking you to do it. Pray, fast, and seek the counsel of God before you give us an answer.

We have burdens to bear but we must endure hardness, as a good soldier of Jesus Christ. *No man that warreth entangleth himself with the affairs of this life; that he may please him who hath chosen him to be a soldier.* We have an advantage against the enemy, it is the word of God and by the word of God we know how to win this war. The word of God puts all of our enemies at great disadvantage against us and by the word of God we know how to deal with this world. We have heard the commandments of our Lord and Savior Jesus Christ and we know the mission we have been called to. We have received power from Jesus Christ to be witnesses of him even unto death all over the world and we shall honor that command. The word of God conquers all our doubt the time has come now that we must hide the word of God in our heart and place our absolute trust in Jesus forever.

Many have been persecuted for the faith in America but what is coming upon us next is far worse than what we have seen. Children as satan sits on his throne manipulating the hearts of men don't be deceived, follow Christ as you have been taught! Let the Word of God be your guide wherever you go and always trust in its power. *For the word of God is living and powerful, and sharper than any **two-edged sword**, piercing even to the division of soul and spirit, and of joints and marrow, and is a discerner of the thoughts and intents of the* *heart.* The Word of God will cut away the poison and at the same time will heal all afflicted by the poison; it puts to death and brings to life; it is the Word of God. Jesus will always be in charge and don't forsake the power of the two-edged sword. Don't abandon the Word of God for a weak and compromised religion that is based on the favor of man! God will never abandon you, he will never leave you, nor forsake you, and knowing this you will be able to boldly say the Lord is my helper and I will not fear what man shall do unto me!

My children we have all decided to give our life to the Lord and live for him. This choice has made us a problem to the world around us and the dark spirits that inhabit this earth. When under such heavy burden as we are now we can either be defeated by giving in to temptation or we can live in victory and our faith can increase. Hard times either break our faith or strengthen our faith. Keep your mind on Jesus Christ and remain in constant communication with him through prayer. Jesus will keep our minds in perfect peace when our minds our fixed on him we must trust him my children. Jesus will continue to supply for us all of our needs almost like hidden manna falling from Heaven that only us believers can see. The doors are open for us as long as we don't compromise our faith. Christ is on our side and trust me no matter what satan throws at us we will be victorious children.

My God my heart is broken but I pray for those who have betrayed us that you have mercy on their souls and they recognize the error of their ways. I pray that they come to Christ and suffer persecution as we do and not be ashamed of their chains as I am not ashamed of mine. I pray for these children that their faith is not compromised and that they hold on to your word no matter what. Even if all men forsake them I pray that they trust in you eternally and always.

Sincerely,

Adam

Lovers of Lies

Then the LORD said unto me, The prophets prophesy lies in my name: I sent them not, neither have I commanded them, neither spake unto them: they prophesy unto you a false vision and divination, and a thing of nought, and the deceit of their heart.-Jeremiah 14:14

To my Sons and Daughters,

The sky is falling, the hills are being crushed, and the oceans have dried up! My America was once a beautiful landscape and now it is a mess that only God can clean up. One nation under God has become one nation under their god and the future of this nation is going down the drain. They have forced us into hiding and imprisoned us for the truth; but before our God one day they will have to explain. Jesus said "God is a Spirit: and they that worship him must worship him in spirit and in truth." The gurus of the temple have perverted the worship of God and have caused people to worship God in ways that he has not prescribed! It sickens me that people who once called themselves believers have indulged themselves in such lewd behavior. Jameson and the others have not only become their teachers but their gods, ruling over the people in place of the true God. The people depend on the gurus for their every move and now I hear that the people bow down before them and kiss their rings. Jesus said "You shall worship the LORD your God, and Him only you shall serve."

Now that the President of New America has been declared the official leader of the Temple of Semiramis, we have no choice but to be ready to protect ourselves. The President's first order of business will be to erect a large watchtower in Brooklyn, New York to prepare the way for the coming Messiah. They've lied to people appealing to their flesh by giving them a false messiah that supposedly they can see but I guarantee none will ever see this man. They claim he is traveling from Jerusalem and he will sit on his throne in Brooklyn ruling the world from his watchtower. They say he shall reign their 1000 years and after that 1000 years he will reveal himself but this is also a lie. What do they have to gain from such lies? The lies they tell are to provide them with money, power, control, money, and more money. They have deceptively manipulated the scriptures to deceive souls.

Behind it all I can see the agenda of Babylon working through the President to use this one nation religion to destroy Israel. The new agenda of the followers of Tammuz is to establish their false christ kingdom in America but in order to do so Israel must be destroyed. They believe that the true Israel is not a country but the people who worship in their temple and therefore the false Israel must be destroyed. There is nothing new under the sun and this isn't the first time that man have claimed to be the savior of the world. If any man comes to you and says that the savior has come and established his reign on earth in secret, mark that person as being misinformed and teach them the truth in love.

Jesus Christ warned us that men would do this over 2000 years ago when he said "If any man shall say unto you, Lo, here is Christ, or there; believe it not. For there shall arise false Christs, and false prophets, and shall shew great signs and wonders; insomuch that, if it were possible, they shall deceive the very elect. Behold, I have told you before. Wherefore if they shall say unto you, Behold, he is in the desert; go not forth: behold, he is in the secret chambers; believe it not. For as the lightning cometh out of the east, and shineth even unto the west; so shall also the coming of the Son of man be." When the true Savior returns to earth to reign and establish his kingdom every eye shall see because he will not hide himself from mankind. We have witnessed men coming to earth before claiming to be God or the savior but eventually it was proven that they were talebearers. Haile Selassie 1, Jim Jones, Matayoshi Jesus, Krishna Venta, Marshall Applewhite, Yahweh ben Yahweh, José Luis de Jesús Miranda, David Koresh, Sun Myung Moon, and many others have claimed to be the Messiah or have been pronounced by others to be the Messiah but it is all lies. My children it is sad to see people swindled out of all their life savings to show complete devotion to the lies of men. The gurus of the temple are in league with satan and have divulged themselves into his deep mysteries of evil.

The moral standard of the people has been corrupted and now every evil desire of the heart has been deemed acceptable. A hedonistic culture has been created, built on the principle that if the followers of Tammuz feel that they are a god then they shall be a god. They have created a culture that says I can do whatever I want to do because I'm god, one day I shall be a god so I can do what I please. The enemy used the leaders of the temple to introduce sexual immorality as an acceptable form of worship and instantly the followers of Tammuz increased. If anybody tells you that you can have a right relationship with God and practice sexual immorality at the same time they are a liar. Polygamy, homosexuality, bestiality, fornication, adultery, pornography, pedophilia, and any other form of sexual behavior outside of marriage between one man and one woman is sin and without repentance salvation is impossible.

For years the church was rocked by the scandals of those who held the position of church leaders but were secretly engaged in sexual perversion. The reputation of the church was damaged, people were hurt, and the world judged the church. Then something strange began to happen the church began to embrace sexual immorality and began to excuse the lifestyles of its leaders and the world observed. When we stood up against sexual immorality we were seen as people that refused to get with the times and then they would point to the churches that taught sexual immorality was a part of life. Behold it is written in the word of God:

"Do you not know that the unrighteous will not inherit the kingdom of God? Do not be deceived. Neither fornicators, nor idolaters, nor adulterers, nor homosexuals nor sodomites, nor thieves, nor covetous, nor drunkards, nor revilers, nor extortioners will inherit the kingdom of God."

They labeled us hateful but it wasn't us that made the rules it was our God he wrote the book and for that our God was made public enemy #1. We are instructed to hate sin and to help the sinner gain freedom from the bondage of sin. Sexual immorality is no different than any other sin and the cure for all sin is repentance. Those who practice sin must make a lifestyle change by taking their sinful lifestyle to the cross and putting it to death. Then a person must begin a new life by picking up their cross and following after Jesus Christ. We rejoice with those who make that journey and we hold nothing against those who reject the gospel but yet they hate us still.

My God is my witness not an ounce of hate is in my blood for those lost in sin for I was once lost in pornography and fornication but God cleansed my soul and I want that freedom for others. Jameson has pulled no stops and the wicked ones who pull his strings have instructed him and others well. By using sexual immorality as bait they have created a religion where free love and sex is acceptable. They live by the doctrine of the evil Aleister Crowley "they do what they will and that is their whole law." If those engaged in sinful lifestyles don't repent then death and suffering shall be their payment. *Woe to those who call evil good, and good evil; Who put darkness for light, and light for darkness; Who put bitter for sweet, and sweet for bitter!*

The poison is spreading to the prisons we are seeing men pledge allegiance to Tammuz by crawling on their hands and feet across the prison yard to show their total devotion. Wooden crosses being burned and the ashes placed on men's foreheads for protection. Men starving themselves of meat to prove how committed they are to their hidden savior. The hours of the mindless chanting and attempts to evoke the spirits of their protectors in dimly lit rooms and many more things have I observed since the temple meetings began in prison. Day by day we are seeing Muslims, Buddhist, Atheist, Mormons, Scientologist, and others forsake the gods of their fathers and join the temple. Your grandmother tells me that your father and Mark have also joined the temple be very careful around them. I pray for your safety and I ask that you pray for Pastor Timothy's strength because he has many things on his heart these days. Kiss your grandmother for me, hug Mark, hug your father and tell him that I love him very much. Continue praying for Peter in Mexico and keep the faith.

Heavenly Father your word says "For whatsoever is born of God overcometh the world: and this is the victory that overcometh the world, even our faith. Who is he that overcometh the world, but he that believeth that Jesus is the Son of God?" The world is closing in us and we ask for you to keep your promise in this life or the next. Save us from the worst of these days as it is hard now for us to endure the things that are transpiring. We love you Lord Glory be to your divine will and your name.-Amen

Sincerely,

Adam

One Name

That at the name of Jesus every knee should bow, of those in

heaven, and of those on earth, and of those under the earth-

Philippians 2:10

To Pastor Timothy,

For years I have sat in this prison dreaming of white sand beaches, palm trees, and beautiful blue skies. I would trade everything in the world just to see the sunrise one more time but now I have different dreams. My thoughts have turned from spacious skies, amber waves of grain, and purple mountain majesties above the fruited plain to vengeance. It has been days since I have seen you at work and today I received the strangest letter from my son Arnold and before my emotions get the best of me Timothy I need to know the truth. Is it true that the B.A.D ambushed the church meeting and opened fire on all of those defenseless people? Is it true that my grandson Mark is missing? Is it true that amongst the hundreds that died due to the recent attacks that my youngest granddaughter Wendy and my wife were martyred? Are there any words that can describe the hurt I feel? Are there any dictionaries that contain such emotions? If I could lose control for one moment then this would be that moment and the outcome would not be peaceful. I'm human and every now and then God allows situations to arise to show me how far that he has brought me from. I haven't spoken to my son in years Timothy so imagine the betrayal I feel receiving a letter from my son bragging pledging his allegiance to Tammuz. Imagine how I feel receiving a letter from my son stating that he made Mark stand there and watch his grandmother and sister be murdered and promised him that if he ever became a Christian he would suffer the same fate. My son has hatred in his heart towards me and my God and I know that somehow Jameson has manipulated that bitterness inside him and others. We have become the objects of human sacrifice to appease the gods of Babylon and great pain has been dealt to the church. Seeing that you have been absent from work is proof enough that something has transpired but I still have hope that all of these things are nothing more than lies and the church is still safe. Honestly, I'm not even sure if you're alive but I hope that Officer Thomas can get this letter to you safely and that all is well with you. These are trying times

Timothy but remember this is the closest to hell that we will ever be. As much as our hearts hurt we can never wish hell on any of our tormentors it is and always will be our job to preach the gospel to all men. Vengeance belongs to God and those who torment us, mock us, jail us, and if they don't repent it will be to their own torment. They laugh at us and say that our God is not coming back for us *but the Lord is not slack concerning His promise, as some count slackness, but is longsuffering toward us, not willing that any should perish but that all should come to repentance.*

Our God is coming for us Timothy but for now we must strengthen what remains of the church. My grandchildren are now your children and you are now their father. My prayer is that you will raise them for the glory of the Lord. Find my grandson Mark and comfort him he has been through a lot recently and I don't want the same bitterness that consumed his father to consume him. Be watchful my son for I have got word that Arnold has betrayed you also an informed the Warden of your actions as well. The fight is truly being brought to us now but all of these things that are happening now are nothing more than distractions. It is important that the church be reestablished and more souls be added to the Kingdom of Heaven. It is not important that Jameson, New Babylon, New America, B.A.D., and my son Arnold have all declared us enemies. We have to stay on track the attacks of the enemy are nothing more than distractions. We must keep our faith in God and allow him to quench all the fiery darts of the wicked one. As the word of God says *"**No weapon formed** against you shall prosper, And every tongue which rises against you in judgment You shall condemn. This is the heritage of the servants of the LORD, And their righteousness is from Me," Says the LORD."*

Let God deal with our enemies and let us complete the task that God has set us on which is preaching the gospel. It is clear to me now that if we continue to focus on these attacks we will lose sight on preaching the true gospel of Christ and we must not lose our focus. The Temple of Semiramis is growing in numbers daily but the whole movement is dead spiritually. They have been deceived into thinking that they are strong because of their numbers but in reality they are weak and their future is very dim. They gather in their temple worshipping in flesh and lies but we will gather together and worship our God in spirit and in truth. I've seen churches die in my lifetime because they lost focus but that will not be the case with this church.

We will not teach an incomplete truth, and we will not allow the work that God began in this church to end without completing the job He called us to do. We will not neglect the scriptures to teach against the culture and we will not look at our numbers and begin to believe the name of our church is more important than God's name. The power is in God even if there are only 4 members left in our church, his name is more powerful than all names and his mission will continue until we join him.

We can't lose focus of who we are in Christ because that is how the church will die and trust me I've seen it happen before. I once had a best friend who had a mega church filled with members, beautiful classrooms, nice location, and programs running all week. The church was the talk of the town and people from all over the country would come and visit his church because of the way he spoke and dressed. At first my buddy really taught from the word of God but as the members increased so did the revenue and so did his circle of friends. His name began to increase, his reputation began to flourish, and his ego began to grow and the problems began. The change was subtle at first I hadn't noticed any difference in him other than he was becoming famous but if I had noticed I would have warned him as a true friend should. It wasn't until one of his ministers was involved in a scandal that I was able to see what was truly going on and by then it was too late. This particular minister in his church just so happen to be a well known singer and had a lot of influence in the church and a lot of connections outside of the church which translated into more revenue, more fame, and more members for my friend's church.

The word of God called for discipline but rather than remove this singer from his office of ministry my buddy simply swept it under the rug. Forgiveness and grace are good but discipline is necessary and in my friends heart he knew that he made the wrong decision but how could he risk losing so much. My buddy trusted in his own name to supply the needs of the church and he had forgotten that it is God who is the head of the church and he gives the increase. Within a few years his church had increased tremendously but the culture had also changed from pleasing God to pleasing mankind. People began to have open sexual affairs in the church but the dangers of fornication, lust, adultery, and homosexuality weren't taught because it might offend someone. So instead grace and financial success was taught and the people flocked to his ministry because it tickled their ears.

They would brag in the streets because they finally had a preacher who tells them what they want to hear which is "God knows their heart so he understands." My brother had neglected the heart of God and although God knew the peoples heart they didn't know Gods heart at all. My buddy had died spiritually and the more I talked to him in private about his ways the more he blasted me publically because he thought that I was jealous of his success. My buddy had exchanged the word of God for fame and once the movie deals, music video cameos, TV show appearances poured in he began teaching more of the world and less of God's word.

The people who didn't know any better bought into it and they adopted his philosophy and they all began to do as they felt in their own heart and it was right because my buddy the famous Life Coach/Spiritual Advisor/ Bishop/Dr./Pastor manipulated scripture to please the people and he became their god. When it was revealed to his congregation that he was involved in several illicit sexual affairs the congregation praised him more and defended him to death. I loved my buddy and I never turned my back on him. I watched in prayer as he lay in the hospital dying of aids complications all alone. He suffered as the church he built forgot about him and praised his younger apprentice for being a better leader. I sat by his bed and gave him the word of God and we prayed and he asked God to forgive his sins and he died right there and he was only a few years over 40. He was my friend but his emerging church and all of its philosophies and questioning if truth really exist did him more harm than good. Without truth my buddy lacked the ability to love his congregation properly so without even noticing it, he taught them to do what they like rather than to do what God had desired.

When I was a child my uncle was a Pastor and our family would go to his church every now and then. I remember it being a small church where everybody knew one another. My uncle taught the word of God faithfully and to say that people had a good time at his church would be an understatement. The church would have fish fry's and bake sales and the worship music was unbelievable. People came and visited that small church just to be blessed by a song from the worship team. The church was small and since it was small my uncle was able to be there for everybody anytime there was a problem. This eventually became a problem for him because people put him on a pedestal and believed that only he could solve their problems. Rather than pray they called my uncle, rather than study they called my uncle, rather than seek God they sought my uncle and he became their god. He began to rule over those people telling them where to buy a house, what jobs to take, and who to marry. I honestly don't believe it was his intention to rule over the people like this but they asked him questions and he felt the need to answer every last question. My uncle had lost focus; he forgot to point people to God. My Uncle's quiet time with Lord disappeared and his studying had declined because he was always doing for the people and he had no time to fellowship with God on his own. My uncle tried to find help but people always wanted his help and somehow someway he began this dangerous ministry where he began to appoint spiritual gifts unto people. God had never told my Uncle these things my uncle had been buttered up by these people and before him they pretended to display certain qualities only because they wanted a title and a position.

The people seen the power my Uncle possessed and they lusted after it because if my uncle had this much power they wanted it too. There was a elder in my uncle's church who wanted to take over the church by any means necessary so he poisoned the ministry. My uncle wasn't the most learned man in the scriptures so the elder used my uncle's lack of knowledge to his advantage. Within a matter of months this elder had destroyed my uncle's ministry and made him look like a fool before the congregation. The sermons grew more confusing each week, guest speakers were allowed to commandeer the pulpit and teach heresy, and my poor uncle grew sick. The ironic thing is the whole time the elder praised my uncle with flatteries he badmouthed him before the congregation criticizing his lack of teaching and leadership. Eventually my uncle's small church grew so small that it died. I remember visiting there one Sunday and my uncle was preaching to my aunt and two other women and I cried like a baby that day.

Pastor Timothy I say this with all respect and love as the Pastor goes so does the church so stay sharp and keep focus. I know that you are under stress because I am under stress but we must trust God and lead his people. This is not the time to make a retreat nor to concede and accept defeat we must fight until our last breath. New Babylon and the Temple cannot and will not be the focus of our church. We will focus on Christ and Christ alone. We have been given a mission to teach the word of God and to proclaim his name to those who are lost. If we take our eyes off of Christ in order to give attention to the work of satan then we will be wrong and I refuse to take part in it. Many of the underground churches have dedicated their services to exposing the evils of New Babylon and the Temple. In the end these churches will die because the work of the Holy Spirit is incomplete. These churches have neglected teaching the scriptures line by line precept upon precept and have opted to teach about conspiracies, theories, hidden messages in popular culture, and how the workings of New Babylon are destroying our society. Teach the scriptures, live by the scriptures and don't be distracted by the work of the enemy. I can see the face of Jameson in my mind laughing at those churches licking his lips because those members are ripe for the picking. Jesus always stuck to his Father's business and his word no matter what was going on around him. Jesus was never distracted by the evil of this world and we must be about our Father's business now. In these last and evil days we have one mission to prepare souls for the coming of the Lord now let's get to it.

Jesus prepare our hearts for your work and keep us focused on the task at hand-Amen

Sincerely,

Adam

The Eulogy

The righteous perishes, And no man takes it to heart; Merciful

men are taken away, While no one considers That the righteous is

taken away from evil.-Isaiah 57:1

To my Sons and Daughters,

Death is unnatural; it is an interruption of life. Death never existed until sin came into the world and death is a result of the curse. God promised to Adam that if he ate the fruit from the forbidden tree that he shall surely die but he never told Adam the extent of that death. Many people ask God if he knew they would eat from the tree why put the tree in the garden? The truth is the tree is not the problem because with or without the tree mankind is a sinner. Take a good look in the mirror my children because the sin is in our hearts and we make the commitment everyday to disobey the word of God. For us to blame our sin nature on a tree is to blame gun related deaths on the gun when in reality it is the man behind the gun that is the cause. The tree was simply an instrument used for our pleasure to carry out our sin of disobedience and we all have a forbidden tree in our life. God promised all mankind that disobeying his word results in death. Although the curse began with Adam it is all of our faults and not just his. Each and every one of us are personally responsible for the sins that we commit and being born in a sinful world we naturally mimic the nature of a fallen people. What I do know is that God never intended for his people to die but at least he gave his life in exchange for ours to end the curse. I can see Jesus now weeping before the grave of Lazarus while the crowd looked on. Weeping because the world he created has fallen and the people he loves must endure the tragedy that comes with losing a loved one.

Where do we go from here after losing a beautiful child and a loving grandmother? Where do we go now? Do we blame God or do we blame their murderers? Couldn't God have done something more to protect them? God is not to blame it is sin that murdered them. The sin that lies in the hearts of their murderers, the sin that lies in the heart of the devil, and the sin that lies in us all. God could've done more he could've protected them but I believe he has because they are free from the evils of this world. Consider that they have been taken away from all the evil that we face today and have been given rest for all eternity. I sit in this prison cell jealous of them because I still suffer for my Lord and they have been blessed to rest with him. Jesus went to the cross for the sins of the world. Jesus was bloodied, bruised and disfigured beyond recognition for our sins. Jesus was betrayed by his closest friends, abandoned by his followers, and betrayed by the government.

From the cross our naked bloody savior said **"It is finished!"** The debt for our sins has been paid and the curse of sin has been destroyed. Family we can mourn for our loss but we can only rejoice for what your grandmother and sister have gained. The word of God has declared "For we know that if our earthly house, *this* tent, is destroyed, we have a building from God, a house not made with hands, eternal in the heavens. For in this we groan, earnestly desiring to be clothed with our habitation which is from heaven, if indeed, having been clothed, we shall not be found naked. For we who are in *this* tent groan, being burdened, not because we want to be unclothed, but further clothed, that mortality may be swallowed up by life. Now He who has prepared us for this very thing *is* God, who also has given us the Spirit as a guarantee. So *we are* always confident, knowing that while we are at home in the body we are absent from the Lord. For we walk by faith, not by sight. We are confident, yes, well pleased rather to be absent from the body and to be present with the Lord." Our loved ones have made a journey that we all will make someday either by earthly death or by the rapture. I am confident that Heaven will be our final destination and the end of our suffering.

But as it is written, Eye hath not seen, nor ear heard, neither have entered into the heart of man, the things which God hath prepared for them that love him.-1 Corinthians 2:9

Sincerely,

Adam

Exodus

Brethren, I count not myself to have apprehended: but this one thing I do, forgetting those things which are behind, and reaching forth unto those things which are before, I press toward the mark for the prize of the high calling of God in Christ Jesus. Let us therefore, as many as be perfect, be thus minded: and if in any thing ye be otherwise minded, God shall reveal even this unto you.-Philippians 3:13-15

To my Sons and Daughters,

The night is far spent, the day is at hand: let us therefore cast off the works of darkness, and let us put on the armor of light. My time of departure has come and soon I will make my last stand against this cruel world. The order has been signed, the decree has been set forth that all Christians in New America shall be beheaded for their faith. Babylon has succeeded in taking over New America and the lady of liberty has fallen into the ocean. Who will save her? Babylon has given us two options we must recant our faith and pledge allegiance to the Red Dragon or we will be killed. Give me liberty or give me death and in this case my liberty is found in Heaven and death is the road I must take to get there. The devil believes that when faced with these odds we will choose our own lives over the will of God, but God will use our lives to prove the devil and the world wrong. We shall die on our feet for Jesus before we live on our knees for satan! GIVE ME LIBERTY OR GIVE ME DEATH!

Our fate is in the hands of God. Mexico has sealed up its borders and is deporting New Americans that try and cross the border but this is where you must run. Years ago I joined a missionary group that would travel to Mexico establishing churches and there is a church in Enredira, Mexico my buddy Fernando whom they call "the fisherman" will be your guide. Pastor Timothy has made all the arrangements for your departure. Mark there is a job down there for you and your younger brother Silas near Castro's fishing camp as deep sea fisherman upon the ship named Bethlehem. New Babylon can't stop us from preaching the gospel because Jesus has set an open door before us to enter the kingdom of heaven and to share the kingdom of heaven on earth with all who will listen. Tremendous opportunities will present themselves for you to help others and you will begin to see that God has taken control over your life and it is no longer your will but his will that is done.

From day to day you will never know or understand what lies ahead but trust in God because divine appointments will happen constantly, so stay in prayer and be ready. My children nobody will be able to stop the will of God in your life, nobody will be able to close the door of opportunity so never mind their distractions just keep focused on the task at hand. There are those who will hinder us in the ministry and try to knock us down but no matter what they throw at you understand that God has already prepared you for it so stay focused. I have seen many of my brothers who came here in chains and have turned their back on God because they felt they no longer had a purpose. I have also seen men who refused the gospel at first but have later come to the faith and have been made pillars in the temple of my God.

I have embraced my mission for Christ and understood that if I was to be here in prison then God would be with me. I believed in my heart that God already had a plan for me in prison despite the opposition. I gave no power to the restriction of these chains or how the enemy could put me to death for witnessing. I only stayed focused on Jesus mission and that was how I was able to maintain peace this long. My children you have given me new hope and have made my last days more exciting than my first days…Thank you. You will encounter false believers and workers of deceit on your journey but pay them no mind because the enemy must attack. Be careful in Mexico, there are many churches there that remind me of the last churches in New America before they were outlawed. These churches were neutral, they rejected satan but they never stood up for Christ in times of crisis. They are only concerned with social activities, community projects, and welfare and because of that Christ has rejected them. They bragged about the name of Christ but Christ spewed them out of his mouth and they have deceived themselves. In their own eyes they are prosperous churches and have need of nothing but in the eyes of Christ they are poor, wretched, miserable, blind, and naked.

I challenge you children to always try and see yourself from the eyes of Christ and never through your own mirror. I challenge you children to always let Jesus be the head of the church and never leave him outside the church knocking on the door as some have. Soon my children the enemies of God will be subdued before us and you shall escape the great tribulation that shall bring about the demise of the world. My final words children are words from Christ himself "Go ye therefore, and teach all nations, baptizing them in the name of the Father, and of the Son, and of the Holy Ghost: Teaching them to observe all things whatsoever I have commanded you: and, lo, I am with you always, even unto the end of the world. Amen."

"They Call me Adam"

Benediction

So Christ was once offered to bear the sins of many; and unto them that look for him shall he appear the second time without sin unto salvation.-Hebrews 9:28

To Jameson friend of the world,

When in the Course of human events it becomes necessary for one people to dissolve the political bands which have connected them with another and to forsake those political bands and the laws of the majority and declare that the gospel shall be and always will be the law of mankind. We hold these truths to be self-evident, that all men are created equal, that they are endowed by their Creator with certain unalienable Rights, that among these are Life, Liberty and the pursuit of Happiness. That to secure these rights, the gospel was given to men from the mouth of God with all authority and power. That whenever any sin becomes destructive of these ends, it is the Right of the People to call on Jesus to abolish it, and to institute new Government upon his or her soul. The foundation of the gospel has been built with Jesus own blood as it was him who laid down his life on the cross for the sins of the world. The law of the world has strayed far away from the gospel interrupting its foundation, making a mockery of its creator, and effecting the right of all men to pursue eternal life. History dictates that mankind has been prone to suffer because of sin in the world since the fall of man.

God shall not take away the freewill of all mankind to choose to serve him or not serve him, but it has come clear that man has grown accustomed to pretending to be God. The Divided States of America has sought to take away our right to choose if we will serve God or not. The world has issued out a long train of abuses and usurpations, and it is now our duty as keepers of the gospel message to throw off such Government, and to provide new Guards for their future security. Such has been the patient sufferance of the believers in Christ; and it is now the necessity of Christians to glorify God and call on him to bring down the evil which seeks to constrain our praise. The history of sin in the world and satan is a history of repeated injuries and usurpations, all having in direct object the establishment of an absolute Tyranny over these people of the world let the current facts be submitted.

1. The devil is the father of all lies, a murderer from the beginning, he abides not in the truth, because there is no truth in him.

2. The wages of sin is death and sin has destroyed the world we live in making living conditions subpar for the inhabitants of earth to dwell in.

3. The devil is a deceiver.

Enough is enough we have been enslaved, beaten, murdered, and ridiculed for representing Jesus Christ. No longer will we endure these chains; no longer will we endure this ridicule and if New Babylon wants to bring this fight to us then bring it because we represent the King. New America has turned its back on Israel since joining New Babylon and the new global agenda is to overthrow Israel and establish one large New Temple in Jerusalem. Jameson you know better than most the time that was spoken of by Daniel the prophet is almost fulfilled. 483 out of 490 years have already come to pass and there are only seven years left on the prophetic timetable. These last seven years will be the worst time on earth reserved for judgment upon the world for their rejection of the Messiah and the opening of Israel's eyes that they may recognize Jesus Christ as the Messiah. Many of our believers have died but they are not forgotten. They are already with Christ and one day they will come back with Christ to rescue believers before the last seven years begins. In the words of Paul the Apostle of Jesus Christ "I do not want you to be ignorant, brethren, concerning those who have fallen asleep, lest you sorrow as others who have no hope. For if we believe that Jesus died and rose again, even so God will bring with Him those who sleep in Jesus. For this we say to you by the word of the Lord, that we who are alive *and* remain until the coming of the Lord will by no means precede those who are asleep. For the Lord Himself will descend from heaven with a shout, with the voice of an archangel, and with the trumpet of God. And the dead in Christ will rise first. Then we who are alive *and* remain shall be caught up together with them in the clouds to meet the Lord in the air. And thus we shall always be with the Lord."

All those that will have died before Jesus comes back for his church will immediately be taken to the Father's house *for to be absent from the body is to be present with the Lord.* Jesus Christ said "Let not your heart be troubled: ye believe in God, believe also in me.

In my Father's house are many mansions: if it were not so, I would have told you. I go to prepare a place for you. And if I go and prepare a place for you, I will come again, and receive you unto myself; that where I am, there ye may be also. And whither I go ye know, and the way ye know." This day will come upon the world suddenly without warning, without sign, like a thief in the night unexpectedly Jesus will reveal himself in the air. Those who have died before this event will return with him and those who are still alive on earth when this event happens will suddenly be called into the air with him. Together as one body of Christ we will journey to the Father's house and the world will have no clue as to where we have gone. The glorious part of this ascension is that we shall all be changed given new bodies and all those who died before this event their physical bodies shall also be called up and joined with them and changed.

But someone will say, "How are the dead raised up? And with what body do they come?" Foolish one, what you sow is not made alive unless it dies. And what you sow, you do not sow that body that shall be, but mere grain—perhaps wheat or some other *grain.* But God gives it a body as He pleases, and to each seed its own body. All flesh *is* not the same flesh, but *there is* one *kind of* flesh of men, another flesh of animals, another of fish, *and* another of birds. *There are* also celestial bodies and terrestrial bodies; but the glory of the celestial *is* one, and the *glory* of the terrestrial *is* another. *There is* one glory of the sun, another glory of the moon, and another glory of the stars; for *one* star differs from *another* star in glory. So also *is* the resurrection of the dead. *The body* is sown in corruption, it is raised in incorruption. It is sown in dishonor, it is raised in glory. It is sown in weakness, it is raised in power. It is sown a natural body, it is raised a spiritual body. There is a natural body, and there is a spiritual body. And so it is written, *"The first man Adam became a living being."* The last Adam *became* a life-giving spirit. However, the spiritual is not first, but the natural, and afterward the spiritual. The first man *was* of the earth, *made* of dust; the second Man *is* the Lord from heaven. As *was* the *man* of dust, so also *are* those *who are made* of dust; and as *is* the heavenly *Man,* so also *are* those *who are* heavenly. And as we have borne the image of the *man* of dust, we shall also bear the image of the heavenly *Man.* Now this I say, brethren, that flesh and blood cannot inherit the kingdom of God; nor does corruption inherit incorruption. Behold, I tell you a mystery: We shall not all sleep, but we shall all be changed in a moment, in the twinkling of an eye, at the last trumpet. For the trumpet will sound, and the dead will be raised incorruptible, and we shall be changed. For this corruptible must put on incorruption, and this mortal *must* put on immortality.

Jameson tell the world Jesus Christ died on the cross bloody and bruised for the sins of the world. Tell the world that he laid in the grave for three days but he was resurrected after those three days and this is the same thing that will happen to all of us who die before he appears. Jameson tell the world that our absence is the least of their concerns because Jesus is coming back and the last seven years on earth until he comes will be hell on earth full of terrible punishment and tragedy for all that rejected him. When the seven years is complete Christ will return again and so will I and all of those who died believing in him and the world will see Him when he returns and they won't be surprised.

The second coming of Christ will be glorious and he shall judge the earth of their sins and establish his kingdom on earth and we shall reign with him 1000 years on this earth. I could write for days about the future but I only write to give you one final chance at repenting for your sins and telling the world the truth about Christ. Christ shall rescue his church from the wrath to come but I can't say the same for the world. For God hath not appointed us to wrath, but to obtain salvation by our Lord Jesus Christ. The world has claimed its independence from God and one day God will claim his independence from the world eternally but until then you still have a chance to change.

Laugh now Jameson, laugh now people of the world, laugh now satan for this will be your last chance to laugh. Mark this day as the beginning of the end for the sad truth is this is the best your life will ever be. There is a day coming when the books shall be opened and all those whose name is not written in the Lamb's book of life shall be judged for their sins. The price for your sin is eternal death and your eyes shall open one day in hell.

Are the pleasures of this world so important to you that you're willing to spend eternity in hell? Is this what your life is worth? Why have you aligned your hearts with satan do you not understand what the scriptures say of his fate?

"Then I saw an angel coming down from heaven, having the key to the bottomless pit and a great chain in his hand. He laid hold of the dragon, that serpent of old, who is *the* Devil and Satan, and bound him for a thousand years; and he cast him into the bottomless pit, and shut him up, and set a seal on him, so that he should deceive the nations no more till the thousand years were finished. But after these things he must be released for a little while. And I saw thrones, and they sat on them, and judgment was committed to them. Then *I saw* the souls of those who had been beheaded for their witness to Jesus and for the word of God, who had not worshiped the beast or his image, and had not received *his* mark on their foreheads or on their hands. And they lived and reigned with Christ for a thousand years. But the rest of the dead did not live again until the thousand years were finished. This *is* the first resurrection. Blessed and holy *is* he who has part in the first resurrection. Over such the second death has no power, but they shall be priests of God and of Christ, and shall reign with Him a thousand years. Now when the thousand years have expired, Satan will be released from his prison and will go out to deceive the nations which are in the four corners of the earth, Gog and Magog, to gather them together to battle, whose number *is* as the sand of the sea. They went up on the breadth of the earth and surrounded the camp of the saints and the beloved city. And fire came down from God out of heaven and devoured them. The devil, who deceived them, was cast into the lake of fire and brimstone where the beast and the false prophet *are*. And they will be tormented day and night forever and ever. Then I saw a great white throne and Him who sat on it, from whose face the earth and the heaven fled away. And there was found no place for them. And I saw the dead, small and great, standing before God, and books were opened. And another book was opened, which is *the Book* of Life. And the dead were judged according to their works, by the things which were written in the books. The sea gave up the dead who were in it, and Death and Hades delivered up the dead who were in them. And they were judged, each one according to his works. Then Death and Hades were cast into the lake of fire. This is the second death. And anyone not found written in the Book of Life was cast into the lake of fire."

This is no laughing matter my dear old friend I pray that you repent and that you tell the world the truth before it is too late. If it seem evil unto you to serve the Lord then choose this day whom you will serve. Will you serve satan and the false deities of Babylon but as for me and my house we shall serve the Lord. What more can I say?

I'm at a loss for words but I pray the truth of scriptures can persuade your heart. Before you there is a choice to make hell or Heaven what will you choose? As for me and my house our fate has been decided. I pray that this final word of God can persuade you.

"Then I saw a new heaven and a new earth: for the first heaven and the first earth were passed away; and there was no more sea. And I John saw the holy city, new Jerusalem, coming down from God out of heaven, prepared as a bride adorned for her husband. And I heard a great voice out of heaven saying, Behold, the tabernacle of God is with men, and he will dwell with them, and they shall be his people, and God himself shall be with them, and be their God. And God shall wipe away all tears from their eyes; and there shall be no more death, neither sorrow, nor crying, neither shall there be any more pain: for the former things are passed away. And he that sat upon the throne said, Behold, I make all things new. And he said unto me, Write: for these words are true and faithful. And he said unto me, It is done. I am Alpha and Omega, the beginning and the end. I will give unto him that is athirst of the fountain of the water of life freely. He that overcometh shall inherit all things; and I will be his God, and he shall be my son. But the fearful, and unbelieving, and the abominable, and murderers, and whoremongers, and sorcerers, and idolaters, and all liars, shall have their part in the lake which burneth with fire and brimstone: which is the second death. And there came unto me one of the seven angels which had the seven vials full of the seven last plagues, and talked with me, saying, Come hither, I will shew thee the bride, the Lamb's wife. And he carried me away in the spirit to a great and high mountain, and shewed me that great city, the holy Jerusalem, descending out of heaven from God, Having the glory of God: and her light was like unto a stone most precious, even like a jasper stone, clear as crystal; And had a wall great and high, and had twelve gates, and at the gates twelve angels, and names written thereon, which are the names of the twelve tribes of the children of Israel: On the east three gates; on the north three gates; on the south three gates; and on the west three gates. And the wall of the city had twelve foundations, and in them the names of the twelve apostles of the Lamb. And he that talked with me had a golden reed to measure the city, and the gates thereof, and the wall thereof. And the city lieth foursquare, and the length is as large as the breadth: and he measured the city with the reed, twelve thousand furlongs. The length and the breadth and the height of it are equal. And he measured the wall thereof, an hundred and forty and four cubits, according to the measure of a man, that is, of the angel. And the building of the wall of it was of jasper: and the city was pure gold, like unto clear glass. And the foundations of the wall of the city were garnished with all manner of precious stones. The first foundation was jasper; the second, sapphire; the third, a chalcedony; the fourth, an emerald; The fifth, sardonyx; the sixth, sardius; the seventh, chrysolyte; the eighth, beryl; the ninth, a topaz; the tenth, a chrysoprasus; the eleventh, a jacinth; the twelfth, an amethyst. And the twelve gates were twelve pearls: every several gate was of one pearl: and the street of the city was pure gold, as it were transparent glass. And I saw no temple therein: for the Lord God Almighty and the Lamb are the temple of it. And the city had no need of the sun, neither of the moon, to shine in it: for the glory of God did lighten it, and the Lamb is the light thereof. And the nations of them which are saved shall walk in the light of it: and the kings of the earth do bring their glory and honour into it. And the gates of it shall not be shut at all by day: for there shall be no night there. And they shall bring the glory and honour of the nations into it. And there shall in no wise enter into it any thing that defileth, neither whatsoever worketh abomination, or maketh a lie: but they which are written in the Lamb's book of life. And he shewed me a pure river of water of life, clear as crystal, proceeding out of the throne of God and of the Lamb. In the midst of the street of it, and on either side of the river, was there the tree of life, which bare twelve manner of fruits, and yielded her fruit every month: and the leaves of the tree were for the healing of the nations. And there shall be no more curse: but the throne of God and of the Lamb shall be in it; and his servants shall serve him: And they shall see his face; and his name shall be in their foreheads. And there shall be no night there; and they need no candle, neither light of the sun; for the Lord God giveth them light: and they shall reign for ever and ever. And he said unto me, These sayings are faithful and true: and the Lord God of the holy prophets sent his angel to shew unto his servants the things which must shortly be done. Behold, I come quickly: blessed is he that keepeth the sayings of the prophecy of this book. And I John saw these things, and heard them. And when I had heard and seen, I fell down to worship before the feet of the angel which shewed me these things. Then saith he unto me, See thou do it not: for I am thy fellowservant, and of thy brethren the prophets, and of them which keep the sayings of this book: worship God. And he saith unto me, Seal not the sayings of the prophecy of this book: for the time is at hand. He that is unjust, let him be unjust still: and he which is filthy, let him be filthy still: and he that is righteous, let him be righteous still: and he that is holy, let him be holy still. And, behold, I come quickly; and my reward is with me, to give every man according as his work shall be. I am Alpha and Omega, the beginning and the end, the first and the last. Blessed are they that do his commandments, that they may have right to the tree of life, and may enter in through the gates into the city. For without are dogs, and sorcerers, and whoremongers, and murderers, and idolaters, and whosoever loveth and maketh a lie. I Jesus have sent mine angel to testify unto you these things in the churches. I am the root and the offspring of David, and the bright and morning star. And the Spirit and the bride say, Come. And let him that heareth say, Come. And let him that is athirst come. And whosoever will, let him take the water of life freely. For I testify unto every man that heareth the words of the prophecy of this book, If any man shall add unto these things, God shall add unto him the plagues that are written in this book: And if any man shall take away from the words of the book of this prophecy, God shall take away his part out of the book of life, and out of the holy city, and from the things which are written in this book. He which testifieth these things saith, Surely I come quickly. Amen. Even so, come, Lord Jesus. The grace of our Lord Jesus Christ be with you all. Amen."

Therefore, the Representatives of Jesus Christ savior of the world do in the Name of Jesus, and by the Authority of the Holy Spirit, solemnly publish and declare, That we are, and of Right are Free from the world and its government but we declare our allegiance and service to God alone. We declare that we are guilty of sin and that death is the price for sin. We also declare that the grace of God has not given us the Hell we deserve but by his mercy his blood was shed to give us the Heaven we don't deserve. Therefore we shall stand before our God exonerated from all guilt because we have an **advocate** with the Father, Jesus Christ the righteous.

He died for our sins and that is the beautiful ugly truth. His love for me was beautiful and flawless and because of that love he allowed himself to become a ugly sacrifice for us all. This is the Declaration of Dependence and for the support of this Declaration, with a firm reliance on the protection of God Almighty, we mutually pledge to each other our Lives, our Fortunes, and our sacred Honor.

They Call me Adam and this is the Beautiful Ugly

After these Things

After this I looked, and, behold, a door was opened in heaven:
and the first voice which I heard was as it were of a trumpet talking
with me; which said, Come up hither, and I will shew thee things
which must be hereafter.
And immediately I was in the spirit: and, behold, a throne was set
in heaven, and one sat on the throne.
And he that sat was to look upon like a jasper and a sardine
stone: and there was a rainbow round about the throne, in sight like
unto an emerald.
And round about the throne were four and twenty seats: and
upon the seats I saw four and twenty elders sitting, clothed in white
raiment; and they had on their heads crowns of gold.
And out of the throne proceeded lightnings and thunderings and
voices: and there were seven lamps of fire burning before the throne,
which are the seven Spirits of God.
And before the throne there was a sea of glass like unto crystal:
and in the midst of the throne, and round about the throne, were four
beasts full of eyes before and behind.
And the first beast was like a lion, and the second beast like a
calf, and the third beast had a face as a man, and the fourth beast was
like a flying eagle.
And the four beasts had each of them six wings about him; and
they were full of eyes within: and they rest not day and night, saying,
Holy, holy, holy, LORD God Almighty, which was, and is, and is to
come.
And when those beasts give glory and honour and thanks to him
that sat on the throne, who liveth for ever and ever,
The four and twenty elders fall down before him that sat on the
throne, and worship him that liveth for ever and ever, and cast their
crowns before the throne, saying,
Thou art worthy, O Lord, to receive glory and honour and
power: for thou hast created all things, and for thy pleasure they are
and were created.

The End